SURF
BETTER

complete
surfing
program

DAVE REARWIN

THANKS

To Chen MeiLing, always, for everything.
To all the surfers, of all ages and places, who just want to surf.
To the Calumet Crew for their advice and encouragement.

Aloha Hawai'i.

Here's to the Ocean

and

To all the surfers, shapers, designers and dreamers
Who took surfing from hand-hewn logs
Through planks and kook boxes
Koa and redwood and balsa
To what we have today.

NOTICE: HEALTH ISSUES

- Anyone starting a physical training program should be certain that they can do so without creating or exacerbating health problems or injuries.
- If you have any medical condition or are under a doctor's care, consult with a physician before starting this or any physical training program.
- If you are doing any part of this program and feel pain or discomfort, stop immediately and consult a physician.

DISCLAIMER: NO MEDICAL ADVICE

The author is not a medical doctor nor a physical therapist, and nothing in this book is to be construed as providing medical advice.

Contents

Make it happen

SURF BETTER: Stronger, Smarter, Longer

This book is for anyone who wants to surf better. The training exercises will help you surf stronger; the information and tips provided will help you surf smarter; the net result is that you can surf better and longer. Not only can you enjoy longer sessions, you can add years to your surfing life.

Some of the tips in this book may seem aimed more at longboarders, others oriented more toward shortboarders, but everything applies to both. In surfing nothing is ever wasted, and longboard or short, the basic principles of the wave are the same. The biggest differences are of degree, not of kind.

Surf Better is an outgrowth of an earlier surfing book, *Secrets of Power Surfing*. Although many readers liked *Secrets* for its surfing stories and its orientation toward attitudes and behaviors, some wished that it had more specific tips and information on waves and on the physical and technical aspects of surfing. *Surf Better* is a response to those requests. *Surf Better* also has a complete Dry Land Surf School section with new surfing training sequences.

Surf Better is divided in four sections. The first section looks at some of the technical aspects and issues involved with surfing: foot placement, backside vs. frontside, and other points that sometimes get overlooked in the heat of the moment. Next, there's a section dealing with the ocean—storms, surf, waves, tides and currents—and what happens when the water meets the shore. The third "how to" section deals with issues related to the surfing spot itself. The final section concentrates on you: training and dry-land practice designed to keep you fit, agile and ready to go when the surf comes up.

The Dry Land Surf School section (Section IV) has over three dozen different surf simulations and other training exercises that you can do singly or in groups. About a dozen of these are vigorous enough to make good "stand alone" mini-workouts when you're in a hurry or just need an exercise break to clear away the cobwebs and get the body working. There's also a 15-minute training package that makes an excellent part of your daily routine; it's short enough to be convenient, and complete enough to keep you in shape and maintain your surfing moves during long layoffs. It's also a good basis for "mix and match" substitutions: you can easily add or subtract different training exercises from the package to get the exact custom program that's right for you.

The surfing training exercises follow a few basic principles:
- Do enough repetitions to increase blood flow and conditioning.
- Improve coordination among interrelated muscle groups.
- Increase range of motion, agility and mobility.
- Avoid wear and tear on joints and connective tissue.
- Do things that will improve your surfing.

Part of surfing better and smarter is making a deliberate effort to improve. To maximize your surfing performance, try to pick one thing to work on every time you surf. Not necessarily every wave, but at least a few times during the session. During one session, it might be popups; during another, it might be foot placement; another time you might concentrate on what you're doing with your knees, or your orientation relative to the wave. Once you've turned an effective technique into a habit, you can forget about it and move on to the next point of improvement.

This is harder than it sounds; it's easy to simply revert to whatever habits you've gotten used to. Even if you're thinking about a technical point during a lull, when the next set appears on the horizon your good intentions seem to evaporate; even if you remind yourself right before you take off, you may finish the wave and realize that somewhere between the first paddle stroke and the time you stood up you got caught up in reacting. One good way to keep focus is to reverse the process: visualize surfing when you're doing the surfing exercises on dry land. Create a bidirectional feedback loop, and you'll progress much faster.

4 Surf Better

PART I: SURFING TECHNIQUE

Center of Gravity: Go with the flow, forward and down

The Takeoff

You should start surfing the wave before you catch it. As the wave approaches, you're already calculating whether it's a left or a right, and whether or not it's going to be a steep or late takeoff. If it's going to be steep or breaking, you'll need to take off at an angle. Too many surfers get fixated on taking off relatively straight, doing a bottom turn, and coming back up the face to get in the pocket. This is a great technique, and on some waves it's necessary, but in other cases it's a recipe for getting wiped out. Sometimes you need an angled takeoff. Don't overdo it; if you're turned too parallel to the wave face, you'll end up in a sideways free-fall.

When paddling, drive your hands at a slight angle out and away from the board, instead of straight back. This is a more efficient motion and will provide more thrust.

Now you're paddling. Just before the wave face reaches you, if you're paying attention you'll notice that the water in front of you appears to become strangely still, as the approaching wave redirects and assimilates the minor constant movements of the standing water into the smooth elliptical motion characteristic of water in a swell.

When this happens, you should give a couple of extra strong strokes and get ready to make your move. If you need to take off at an angle, sometimes it's best to paddle straight (perpendicular to the wave) to maximize your speed relative to the speed of the wave, then make your final adjustment by putting extra energy into the last stroke or two on one side or the other to turn the board in the desired direction.

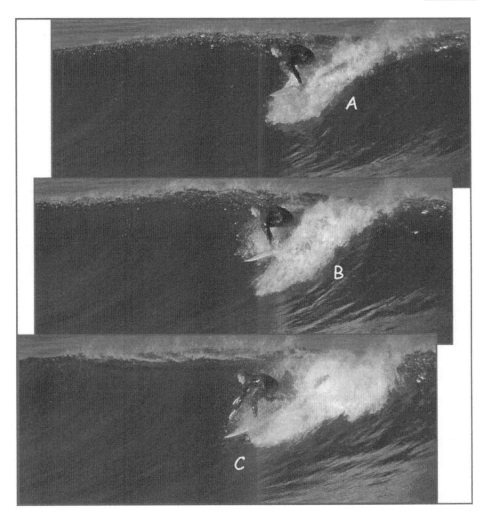

Angle and Weight Distribution

Compare image C above (hips back) with the surfer on page 5 (hips centered). Use weight shift to keep your board at the desired angle.

As you paddle for the wave, be aware of any boils between you and the shore. These may mark the end of the runway, as it were—the point at which the wave is going to jack up and break. A common mistake made by even experienced surfers is to start paddling too soon, the intention being to build up speed. But this risks using up the runway; at some quick-jacking breaks if you take even eight or ten strokes you may be pitched and buried. It's often better to wait until the wave is fairly close, then launch in a "stick and go" motion plus a few very strong strokes. Again, a properly-angled takeoff can mean the difference between success and disaster. The surfer in the picture below took a steep angle, outran the lip, and made the drop.

Late takeoff + reef boil = steep angled drop

Compare the takeoff angle of the surfer above with the one on the preceding page. Adjust your takeoff angle to the steepness of the face and the pitching lip of the wave.

A good popup isn't a matter of leaping to your feet; it's a movement of placing the board beneath your feet. You can also initiate your turn as you pop up. Control the board with your hands until your feet are ready to take over; don't lose the feel of the board at any time.

The action of popping up will cause your board to slow down slightly. On some waves, you can pop up as soon as you feel the board being lifted and driven forward, but on more critical waves the slight loss of forward speed as you pop up can leave you hung up at the top of the wave, set up to be pitched or to free-fall down the face. On these waves it's best to take an extra stroke or two (on really big waves, even more) to get partway down the face before popping up.

As the illustrations above show, you have to stay low—the steeper the wave, the more important it becomes to keep your center of gravity down and the body forward, even if your weight is back. The forward lean isn't as extreme as it often looks; if you drew a straight line from the surfer's board through his feet and on to the top of his head, and then rotated the image so that the board was horizontal you'd see that the position is a balanced crouch. The forward lean is just enough to stay perpendicular to the wave face, plus a couple of degrees more to compensate for the acceleration of the drop.

Foot Position

Regardless of which direction you're going, and regardless of whether or not you're regular (left foot forward) or goofy-foot (right foot forward), the placement of your feet on the board is important. In particular, the position of your feet relative to the centerline is crucial.

Consider the position of your feet on a surfboard, relative to the centerline. There are many stances on a surfboard, ranging from feet parallel and totally sideways across the board to feet facing more or less forward. You can surf with both feet on the centerline, one foot on either side, or both feet more toward one side.

Placement and movement of the back foot seems to be natural for most people: start on the centerline and adjust placement in the direction of the turn, or leave the foot in place and tilt it into the turn. The same is true of the front foot. Use various foot positions depending on the wave and what you're trying to do with it.

The direction of the feet also makes a difference: turning the feet will turn the hips and shoulders in the same direction. The front foot especially can be rotated for fine tuning. The next time you're on a wave, try turning just your front foot in different orientations relative to the board. You don't have to pick it up off the board; just rotate it a bit toward the front or a bit more to the side. Feel how this changes the orientation of your hips and shoulders, and how it affects your interaction with the wave.

In addition to foot placement and orientation, you can use a leg scissor motion both to assist your turns and to jam the rail of your board into the face of the wave. Visualize this the next time you do the scissor exercises (#9, #21) in this book. Use with finesse on the wave; it doesn't take much to make a difference and if you overdo it your foot may slip off the board.

Let's look at how foot placement works in practice. Each of the surfers in the following illustration—one turning backside, one turning frontside—has positioned his front foot to maximize rail control in the direction of the turn. In the upper picture (backside turn), the heel is well to the side of the centerline, toward the inside of the turn. The surfer's weight is naturally transmitted down through the heel to the turning rail. In the lower picture, a frontside turn, the foot is more toward the other side of the centerline, again toward the turn. This allows more weight to be shifted to the rail on the inside of the turn by applying pressure to the ball of the foot.

These are slight differences, but they're important. If the surfer in the lower picture had placed his foot in the same position as the other surfer, it would be hard for him to tilt the board and drive the rail into the face of the wave.

*position front foot
to set rail*

Let's take a more detailed look at various front foot positions, relative to the centerline of the board, and how they work.

The surfers in the topmost images on the following page (A and B) have their front foot with the heel well to the side of the centerline, on the inside of the turn. This makes it easy to turn by simply putting the weight on the heel.

The next two surfers (C and D) initially had their front foot set up for a frontside turn, with most of the foot on the wave side of the centerline. This made it easy to tilt the board and drive the rail into the wave, but to cut back they had to lift the front of their foot to shift their weight back to the other rail.

The surfer in image C also shifted his weight toward the rear of the board, causing the board to stall and slow down. (This can be a useful tactic in some situations, but did not appear to be intentional on this wave, where surfer C was dropping down beneath the pitching lip of a hollow wave—not a good time to lose speed.) An alternative for both surfers would have been to reposition the front foot with a quick motion of an inch or two. And in fact, on the day these pictures were taken, both of these surfers did just that on other waves.

The bottom images show the result of getting too far onto the backside rail. The surfer in image E started the wave intending to go backside, and set up with his front foot on the wave side of the centerline. So far, so good—but when the wave closed out to his left and he tried to change direction, his front foot placement made it impossible to reset the rail for a steep frontside turn. He was in a no-win situation: it was too late to move the front foot without losing speed and board control on the steep, breaking face—but leaving his weight on the front foot to maintain speed made the board tilt the wrong way. Result: he did not make the wave.

foot way off center

can't set rail

Frontside vs. Backside

An amazing number of otherwise competent surfers ride only certain breaks, or go almost exclusively in one direction, because they don't like going backside. In some cases this is more than preference, it's an absolute phobia. If we examine the mechanics of backside vs. frontside surfing and turning, this aversion to backside makes very little sense.

Think for a moment about how your body weight rests on your feet. The bones of your lower leg (tibia and fibula) direct your body weight down to the foot and into the heel. This means that the most natural way to apply pressure to the surfboard is through your heel. Which means that in some situations backside is easier than frontside.

When you're going backside, your heels are on the side of the centerline closest to the wave. This makes it very simple to apply pressure to the "uphill" side of the board (the side toward the wave). This matters because applying pressure in this way lets you use the rail and "uphill" fins (if any) by tilting the board into the face of the wave.

You can do this frontside, of course, but the body mechanics are entirely different, often involving more stressful positions of the legs and upper body. The easiest way to shift your weight toward the face of the wave would be to lean—but the wave is in the way. Extreme knee flexion toward the wave is another option, but you face the same space restrictions. In some cases, on a steep frontside face you can even catch your knee in the wave.

A backside turn, in contrast, allows you to use your hips—your approximate center of gravity (CG)—to shift your weight toward the wave and keep the board tucked firmly into the face. (This involves what skiers call angulation: pushing your hips toward the hill on a steep slope so that the edges of the skis bite and hold.)

Another advantage of a backside wave is that it allows you to easily grab a rail to jam the board even more firmly into the face and hold the line you want on a steep wave.

The pictures on the following page illustrate this. In the upper picture, the surfer going backside is able to keep his center of gravity into the wave by using extreme angulation, adding a rail grab for stability and board control. Because his back is to the wave, he can grab the rail between his feet without difficulty. He can keep both feet solidly on the board, adding to his stability and control.

The frontside surfer on a similar wave at the same break is unable to attain the same degree of rail control without some compromises— notice the stressful position of the rear foot and ankle, where the heel has to come up off the board. Being frontside also places the surfer's front leg in a position that makes it impossible to grab the downhill rail between his feet. His hips, being away from the wave, can't be used to jam the rail of the board into the wave; instead he has to use his head and upper body, leaving his center of gravity farther from the face of the wave.

If you have allowed yourself to slip into unidirectional surfing, make it a point to start riding waves that force you to go the other way. If you spend several sessions going contrary to your preferred direction, you'll find that going one way is, on the whole, neither better nor worse than the other. They are simply different. Each offers certain benefits, and each requires a different technique.

Often something as simple as reorienting your front foot (either by moving it relative to the centerline, or simply turning it more to the front or to the side) can increase your effectiveness instantly, and turn your phobic direction into something to look forward to.

back vs. front:
CG and angulation

*cutback: hip-to-wave location
changes everything*

Then there's the issue of cutbacks. On a backside wave, a cutback is a frontside turn; on a frontside wave, a cutback is a backside turn. The preceding page shows a comparison of two surfers making a similar sharp cutback on a similar wave at the same break.

The body position for the frontside cutback (upper photo) is more extreme, almost upside down. Since the surfer turning frontside can't use his hips (center of gravity) to execute the turn, he has to rely on an extreme position of the upper body to incline the board and control the rail. This puts his CG above the rest of his body—an unstable configuration which can't be maintained for long. To recover, he has to bring his entire upper body back over the board.

In the backside cutback (lower photo) the board is actually at a slightly steeper angle, and yet the surfer is in a much more natural position. He is able to put the board on the rail with relative ease, simply by using his center of gravity (hips) and letting his weight drive through his heels, leaving his upper body vertical. To recover from this position and roll the board back onto the other rail, all he needs to do is drive his knees forward and bring his heels beneath his hips, which will shift his weight to the balls of his feet as he slides the board back beneath his body. (See #18, Hip Lift, in this book.)

In both cutbacks, the upper body is roughly parallel to the deck of the board, and there is a straight line from the hips (center of gravity) through the feet, roughly perpendicular to the surface of the board. The centrifugal force generated by the turning action drives the body toward the board.

FACTOID: BODY POSITION

If you rotate the picture of the frontside cutback (upper photo on the preceding page) about 90° clockwise, so that the board is horizontal, and compare it to the photo of the upright surfer on the cover of this book, you'll find that the body positions are remarkably similar.

Technical Practice Checklist

Here's a short list of observations, techniques and tactics to consider and practice during your surf sessions. Not all of these will apply to every wave. Try to come up with additional items that suit your style.

Pre-takeoff:
- Is the wave a left or a right, or both? Does either direction look more or less feasible (possible close-out, etc.), based on your observations of previous waves?
- Reef boils, if any: catapult and "end of runway."
- How many strokes are you going to need, approximately?

Takeoff and popup:
- Consider takeoff angle, if any.
- Sense the change in water movement as the face arrives.
- Decision: get up high, or paddle down into the pocket?
- Decision: pop all the way up, or stay down in a crouch and grab the rail to jam the board into the face (backside)?
- Offshore wind: pop up low and stay in a "downhill racer" crouch.
- Place the board under your feet: hand the board off from your hands to your feet, like passing a baton.
- Learn to turn as you're popping up, instead of waiting until you're up and then turning.
- Set feet relative to centerline so you can set the rail.
- Longboard: try popping up, cross-step forward to start the drop into the wave, then step back and turn. (Good for getting in early, for staying in waves that back off, and in strong offshore wind.)

The drop:
- Use suitable angle to the peak (left or right).
- Use suitable angle to the face—both you and the board.
- Shift weight to back foot as needed.

- Drive knees forward and into the wave (frontside); angulate with hips and center of gravity into the wave (backside).
- Use leg scissor motion to turn quicker and set the rail harder.
- Keep the feeling of the board through your feet.

Riding:
- While going across the face, try reorienting your front foot to feel the effects (mostly longboard).
- Shift your weight back and forth (front foot – back foot) to change your speed and angle of the board on the face of the wave.
- Don't ride passively; be aware of feeling the board through your feet at all times.
- Longboard: surf on the front 1/3 of your board to get more speed through critical sections. When cross-stepping, don't hurry; take smooth steps up and back. (Helps avoid tripping on your leash.)

Turning:
- Reposition feet as necessary (relative to centerline) to turn, straighten out, or cut back.
- Reorient feet as necessary (pointing more toward the front or toward the side of the board) for frontside or backside turning and riding.
- Use the tail rocker and rail to turn. Try to find the sweet spot just in front of the "uphill" side fin (longboard with 2+1 setup). Apply pressure to the rail above this spot to engage the side fin; since it's angled, it wants to turn up the face and will do so if you engage it.
- Use leg scissor to add to turn.
- Try gently rolling the board from one rail to the other.
- Longboard: try turning while riding the front 1/3 of the board, using the nose rocker to turn.
- Longboard: try moving up and down the face while riding the front 1/3 of the board: flatten the board on the wave to sideslip down, then tilt the board toward the face and use nose rocker to climb the face. (Sideslip may not work if your board has hard down rails in the front 1/3 of the board.)

Leash Management and the "Houdini Moment"

You've probably seem someone trotting down the beach or rushing across a park to the water, only to trip on their own leash. Common sense would indicate that the time to attach your leash is right before going in the water. In fact, your leash can cause problems ranging from trivial to fatal.

On the beach: At one spot, where the shore is rimmed by large, jagged boulders placed there to prevent erosion, a surfer trots across the parking lot and over the topmost boulder, leash attached, hurrying to hit the waves. As he leaps from one boulder down to another, his leash catches on a rock behind him. Result: full face-plant on edge of boulder, broken nose, stitches, and at least one broken tooth.

In the water: You can hook your leash on a rock underwater almost as easily as on shore. In big surf, it's not a pleasant experience. Typically, the leash slips under a submerged rock; you end up on one side of the rock and your board ends up on the other, with the leash running down under the rock—and underwater. In heavy surf, the board is dragged shoreward, pulling you under and wedging your foot and ankle against—or even under—the rock. You can't pull free, you can't come up for air, and you have a very difficult time reaching the Velcro (you're being thrashed around by the surge and your ankle is not very accessible).

It's what you might call a "Houdini moment": you have only about 60 seconds (max) to escape from this situation before the possibility of drowning turns into a reality. This can and does happen; one California surfer drowned on a big day in less than six feet of water when the leash went under a rock and there was no way to get it off.

Once you've experienced a Houdini moment, leash management becomes second nature. But on big days you have some difficult choices: if you're going out at a rocky beach with no channel, so that the only way is to wait for a lull and paddle hard, leaving the leash off is probably safer. However, if your timing is bad and you get caught inside, you face the prospect of losing your board and having it turned to foam chips as the surf batters it against the rocks on shore.

You often face the same choice on the way back in to the beach: if you remove your leash early, to avoid getting tethered to a submerged rock or hog-tied in the shorebreak, you might lose your board. And in big surf and heavy shorebreak, with rips and cross-currents, you might be safer with your board than without it. These are judgment calls that depend on the situation; only you can make them.

PART II: KNOW YOUR OCEAN

What is this wave trying to tell you?

Sea, swell and waves

Even people who have surfed for years and who have gotten very proficient sometimes show an amazing ignorance of the medium in which their sport takes place. This lack of knowledge can create frustrating, unpleasant or downright dangerous situations that are entirely avoidable. You don't need to be an oceanographer, but it does help to have some understanding of what makes surf bigger or smaller, better or worse.

Where do ocean waves come from?

The short answer is "wind." Big or small, clean or junky, every ocean wave (excluding, of course, tsunamis) starts with wind. (This includes backwash, since without a wind-generated wave to start with, there would be no backwash.)

The chain of events is simple. Wind blows, creating irregularities on the surface of the water: ripples, wavelets and chop. These move more or less in the direction of the wind. (You can replicate this by blowing across the surface of a bowl of water.)

The harder the wind blows, the bigger the irregularities (still ripples, wavelets and chop) become; this creates more surface area for the wind to push against, which in turn enlarges the irregularities even more. This feedback loop is enhanced as chop and wavelets created by the wind arrive at smoother water, making it rougher and more susceptible to the effects of the wind. At the same time, opposing forces gradually cancel each other out, while complementary forces are reinforced. The chop begins to coalesce into larger and more well-defined seas. (Think of raindrops flowing down a window; they join together to form larger drops, which flow faster down the glass, picking up smaller droplets as they go.) At some point the random assortments of ripples, wavelets and chop become waves.

Most storms aren't stationary, but move across the surface of the planet. In a moving storm, the largest waves are created in front of the storm, where the wind and the storm are moving in the same direction. In a hurricane or typhoon, the wind moves in a circular pattern and pushes waves out in all directions; the largest waves are those generated in front of the moving storm. However, if a hurricane "stalls" or remains relatively stationary over a point (which sometimes happens with hurricanes below the tip of Baja California, for example) sizeable waves can still be generated.

The three primary factors influencing wave size are wind speed, duration of the storm and fetch (the distance over which the wind blows). The higher the wind speed, the more energy is imparted to the water and the larger the waves become, and as wave height increases, so does the dominant wavelength. The same is true of storm duration: a long-lasting storm has more time to transfer energy to the water, creating larger waves and longer dominant wavelengths. And a storm with high wind speed that moves for a long time in the same direction (long fetch) will create the largest waves of all.

But as with everything, there is a limit. When the waves reach speeds close to that of the wind, the wind can no longer transfer energy to them, and they will not increase in size (except for relatively slight increases as smaller packets of energy are redistributed by combining into larger ones). Wave height is also limited by the ratio of height to wavelength. If the height of a wave reaches about 1/7 of its wavelength, it becomes unstable. The wind will blow the top off (whitecap), which reduces the amount of energy in the wave. When the energy imparted to the waves by the wind is equal to the energy lost by the waves through breaking or other frictional loss, maximum height has been reached. The condition of maximum wave height is called a "fully developed sea."

As wind velocity (v) increases, the **size** of the waves is proportional to the 3rd power of wind speed (v times v times v). The wave **energy** generated by the wind increases even more, to the 4th power of the wind speed, so a 40-knot wind over the ocean generates not double, but 16 times the wave energy of a 20-knot wind.

The graph on the following page depicts the massive increase in energy as wind speed increases. Note that the shaded humps on the graph do NOT represent wave height, but wave energy.

The energy of a wave is proportional to the square of its height, so a 20-foot wave has four times the energy of a 10-foot wave. This makes sense, since a higher wave is also thicker, and its energy extends deeper beneath the surface of the water (as we'll discuss in detail below). In this respect deep-water waves are like icebergs in that only a small portion is visible on the surface.

To summarize what is proportional to what:
- Wave size: wind speed 3rd power (v^3)
- Wave energy: wind speed 4th power (v^4)
- Wave energy: wave height squared (h^2)

The last item (wave energy: proportional to wave height squared) is the one with the most immediate relevance to surfers. When the swell hits, this relationship will affect every wave you ride.

Note also that the higher the wind velocity, the more long-period wave energy is generated. A 20-knot wind (whose energy is represented by the very small dark shape at the bottom of the graph) does not generate any wave period longer than about 12 seconds, and most of its energy is in the 5-8 second period range. To even begin to generate waves with a 20-second period requires about 30 knots of wind velocity, and for solid swells of 20 seconds or more, higher wind speeds are required. And, as we'll see, wave period has a huge effect on the size, quality and power of the surf.

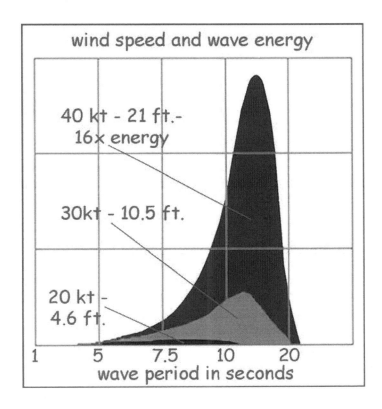

Higher wind speed means more long-period waves

In the chaos and turbulence of a storm, waves of different sizes are generated. The wave energy traveling out from a storm consists of energy packets of various sizes, with different speeds and intervals. The largest waves have the most energy and travel the fastest. When they acquire enough energy, they are traveling faster than the storm and move out of the area of storm-generated wind. We now have a deep-water swell.

Meanwhile, patterns begin to emerge. Sizes become more regular, with the highest one-tenth of all waves being twice as high as the average wave height—and four times more powerful. These biggest $1/10^{th}$ of all waves from a given storm are the ones that will become sets when they reach the surf zone, and the largest $1/100^{th}$ will be cleanup sets. But first a few things have to happen.

As the swell moves across the ocean, the process of energy redistribution continues. The smaller packets of energy (chop and wavelets) are absorbed into the larger packets (the swell). The waves begin to smooth out, and the larger packets of energy (swells) begin to form groups (wave trains) consisting of swells of similar size and frequency. During this process, the redistribution of energy (to larger and larger swells) results in longer and longer distances—and time intervals—from the peak of one swell to the next. The swell becomes smoother and more regular ("cleaner" in surfing terms).

If you hang around surfers in California, you hear a lot of talk about "southern hemi" swells. This refers to swells generated by storms in the Southern Hemisphere, often in the vicinity of New Zealand. What makes these swells special?

Since big waves are generated by storms with strong winds blowing in a constant direction, any area with such winds is a good source of surf. As it happens, the area south of New Zealand meets this description, and the long journey through the open ocean to the eastern Pacific gives the swell plenty of time to organize in regular, long-period wave trains. In addition, there are no island chains obstructing the progress of these swells as they head toward Hawai'i and the West Coast of the United States.

Other sources of long-interval, high-quality surf are typhoons and hurricanes, which form over warm water. Due to their extremely high wind speeds, these disturbances can generate very large long-period swells, especially in front of the storm track. Unfortunately, typhoons and hurricanes often meander in all directions, which scatters the wave energy.

How do waves travel through the ocean?

The sea is filled with apparent contradictions. In the open sea, a deep-water wave train moves at half the speed of the individual waves in the train. This is because in a certain sense, the individual waves don't exist. How can this be? Think back to the redistribution of energy during the formation of a swell. This process continues as the waves form trains and move across the ocean. What we see as a peak or wave crest is simply the result of energy being accumulated at that point.

Individual waves are packets of energy that travel in a cycle of growth, acceleration, and decrease. If we could watch closely a group of waves crossing the sea, we would see waves crests appear at the back of the wave train, move through the train, and disappear at the leading edge of the group. In visualizing this pattern, it may help to think of a spot marked on a roller bearing underneath a moving conveyer belt. As the conveyer belt passes over it, the spot rises, accelerates forward as it heads to the top of the roller, then starts to lose its forward motion as it rotates down toward the bottom of the roller. The whole time the conveyer belt (the wave train) continues to move forward, but each roller bearing stays in place, with individual spots rising and falling, rushing forward and falling back, with each rotation.

And in fact, in a deep water wave the water does not travel forward; only the energy does. Instead, individual water particles move up and down in circular orbits. (They move up the face, forward on the crest, down the backside and backward in the trough.) At the surface, the diameter of these orbits is roughly equal to the wave height. Beneath the surface, the vertical motion decreases until at a depth equal to about ½ the wavelength, there is no vertical motion at all. This area, far below the surface, is the base of the wave. A cross-section of the underwater portion of the wave is shaped like a tall cone with the wide end (bigger circular motion) up and the point (tapering to zero motion at the base of the wave) down.

Again, the depth of a wave (the part underwater) is equal to about ½ the wavelength. This has great significance to surfers:

- Most of a wave—and the vast majority of its energy—is underwater. The part of the wave that is visible is only a tiny portion of the total energy packet.
- Since wave depth is proportional to wavelength and therefore to period, longer period waves have far more power than short period waves, because their underwater "energy cones" are far deeper and have much greater volume. For example:
  - 10-second swell - wavelength 500 feet - depth 250 feet.
  - 17-second swell - wavelength 1500 feet - depth 750 feet!

How fast do waves (or wave trains) travel?

And how long does it take for them to cross the ocean? For calculating the time required for waves to travel a given distance from their source, what matters is the speed of the wave train, not the individual wave. Because of the complexity of the dynamics of surface waves, any calculation is an approximation, but the general concepts remain valid. A wave train with a period of 14 seconds travels at about 25mph in deep water (even though an individual wave might move at approximately 50mph). This wave train would take about 24 hours to travel 600 miles. A group of waves with half the period (7 seconds) would take twice as long.

The implications for surfing are:

1. The longer period swell arrives first (since it travels fastest), therefore
2. The early part of a swell is best, with surf quality deteriorating as the slower, shorter-period wave trains arrive.

When thinking about wave speed, there are several points to consider.

- In deep water (defined as ocean depth deeper than the ½ the wave length), wave speed depends on wave length, which in turn is related to wave period.
- In shallow water (defined as ocean depth less than the ½ the wave length), wave speed depends on ocean depth.
- In deep water, the speed of a wave is directly proportional to the period. For example, a wave with a 20-second period travels twice as fast as one with a 10-second period.
- The speed of the wave (in knots) is about three times the wave period (1kt = 1.15mph). For example:

    10 second interval – Speed 30kt = 35mph
    12 second interval – Speed 36kt = 42mph
    17 second interval – Speed 51kt = 60mph
    20 second interval – Speed 60kt = 70mph

Divide these numbers by 2 to get the approximate speed of the wave train (set) as it crosses open ocean.

These approximate speeds can be used to calculate when swells from a distant storm system might be expected to arrive at your break. Since individual waves travel twice as fast as the wave train (set) they are in, remember to divide the speed by two to get the speed at which the wave trains (sets) are traveling.

Longer period waves not only travel faster in deep water, because of their much greater depth and total energy, in the open ocean they are much less affected by surface turbulence than short-period waves. For example, a short-period (say, 7 second) swell running head-on into a 17-second swell has a relatively small effect. Why? Because the "energy cone" of the 7-second swell is so much smaller. The base of the 17-second swell extends down 750 feet, while the base of the 7-second swell is only about 130 feet down, and is much narrower (and with much less energy) even at the surface. Most of the longer period swell passes under the shorter period swell without being affected.

In shallow water (as we'll examine later in greater detail), it's a different story, and in the surf zone short-period waves have a major impact on even very long-period swells. This is because the large "energy cone" of the longer period waves is reduced as the wave enters shallow water. In addition, the maximum speed of the long period waves is reduced in shallow water. By the time a wave gets to the lineup, the equalizing effect of the ocean floor allows much smaller, shorter-period waves to degrade the surf from a long-period swell. Nevertheless, in general the longer the period, the better the form, in spite of interference.

The longer the period, the longer the time between sets. At the source, wave trains (sets) move at different speeds, with the longer period sets moving faster. Over thousands of miles of travel, a slight difference in speed results in a long wait between the arrival of one set and the next. Just a few one-hundredths of a second difference in period at the source will mean a gap of half an hour 6000 miles away.

The table below summarizes the relationship between period, wave length, wave depth and speed in the open ocean. Notice that wave depth (the underwater base of the wave) is ½ the wave length.

WAVE PERIOD	WAVE LENGTH (approximate)	WAVE DEPTH (approximate)	DEEP WATER SPEED (approximate)
10 seconds	510ft	250ft	35mph
12 seconds	820ft	410ft	42mph
17 seconds	1500ft	750ft	60mph
20 seconds	2100ft	1050ft	70mph

If you're observing waves, get in the habit of estimating the period (number of seconds between waves).   This is far easier than attempting to judge the wave length or speed, and it has a lot of relevance when it comes to surf size, power and quality.

How deep is deep?

In discussions of waves and swell, there are frequent mentions of "deep water" and "shallow water" waves. Waves behave differently in deep water than in shallow water. But how deep is deep, and how shallow is shallow? In physical oceanography, when discussing the behavior of ocean waves the terms "deep" and "shallow" describe not absolute water depth, but the relationship of water depth to wavelength.

Deep water is defined as water whose depth is greater than ½ the wavelength (the distance between two crests). Shallow water means that the water depth is less than ½ the wavelength. (Actually, oceanographers hedge their bet by saying "significantly" greater or less, but the general concept is useful enough.) Why ½ the wavelength? Because this depth, as mentioned earlier, is the base of the wave.

Shallow water, then, is the ocean depth at which the base of the wave begins to be affected by the sea floor.

In deep water, the speed of the wave depends on wavelength (which in turn is related to period). Longer (longer period) waves travel faster.

In shallow water, the speed of the wave depends on the depth of the water. We'll learn more about this when we discuss surf (see section on Wave Changes in Shallow Water).

FACTOIDS: SURFACE WAVES – TSUNAMIS

- *A 60-knot storm lasting for 10 hours makes waves almost 50 feet high in open water.*
- *A far more powerful tsunami, passing under your boat in the open ocean, would be unnoticed; even a massive tsunami is less than one meter (3 feet) high, and due to the extremely long wavelength, which may exceed 60 miles, the crest is no more than an imperceptible slight bulge, almost flat. The period of a tsunami may be over an hour.*
- *Tsunamis, which travel at up to 550 mph, gradually diminish in intensity—but only for a time. They reach a minimum at about 3700 miles from their point of origin, but after that the curvature of the Earth gradually bends the wave fronts to refocus them at about 7500 miles from their starting point.*
- *Even in mid-ocean, tsunamis behave like shallow-water waves. This is due to their great wavelength (often over 100km or 60 miles): since their depth (like that of other waves) is ½ their wavelength (50km or 30 miles) and maximum ocean depth in most regions is only about 11km (7 miles), the base of the tsunami is dragging on the sea floor even in mid-ocean!*

Terminology

- Face: The front of a wave.
- Height: For oceanographers and many surfers, the distance from trough to crest on the face. For Hawaiian surfers, the distance from the still-water line to the crest on the back of a wave.
- Significant Wave Height: The height of the highest 1/3 of the waves observed at a given site. This is the height usually given when overall surf or swell size is estimated.
- Set: Generally the highest 1/10th of the waves observed at a given site. A set may be anywhere from one to a dozen or more waves.
- Cleanup Set: Generally the biggest 1/100th of the waves observed.

- Amplitude: One-half the wave height (i.e., the distance from either the crest or the trough to the still-water line). Surfers don't use this term, but it's a more accurate measurement of wave size than the face, and generally approximates the backside measurement preferred in Hawai'i.
- Closed Out: When surf is breaking all the way across a beach, eliminating any channels. When waves no longer consist of peaks and edges, but huge walls breaking all the way across.
- Fetch: Distance over which the ocean wind is blowing
- Period: The number of seconds it takes for two wave crests to pass a given point.
- Frequency: The number of waves in a given time period.
- Sea: Disorganized waves and chop in the vicinity of a storm.
- Still-Water Line: Sea level; the level of the ocean if there were no waves.
- Swell: Regular waves moving in sine curves across the ocean.
- Wind swell: Same as swell, but created by more local wind disturbances. Shorter period, usually not as clean.
- Wavelength: The distance between the crests of two waves in succession.
- Sideband swell: Secondary swell generated by wind, moving outward at an angle to the direction of the primary swell.
- El Niño (ENSO—El Niño/La Niña-Southern Oscillation): Recurring (up to 5-year interval) climate pattern of surface warming of the tropical eastern Pacific and higher surface air pressure in the western Pacific. La Niña is a name invented to describe the opposite condition: colder ocean in the eastern Pacific and lower air surface pressure in the western Pacific. These changes affect weather, storm patterns and surf worldwide. In 1998, an unusually intense El Niño killed approximately 16% of the world's reef systems by elevating air and sea temperatures. Major ENSO events are occurring with increasing frequency.
- MJO: a short-term (30-60 day) cycle of heavy and light tropical rainfall, which affects tropical cyclone/hurricane formation.

Your Ocean: Love it or lose it

Even though we're aware of the problem of environmental pollution, as surfers we usually don't think we're part of that problem. OK, we do take a boat out to a special break once in a while, maybe at a surf camp, but that's minor, right? Well, maybe (although as they say, every little bit counts), but there's another, more significant issue, one that's involved every day. We tend to believe that surfing itself is a "green" sport, eco-friendly and essentially harmless to the environment. But consider the following facts.

- 400,000: number of new surfboards made each year using toxic foams and synthetic resins.
- 20%: amount of each new board that is thrown away during the shaping process; all of this ends up in landfills, where toxic chemicals leach into the soil.
- 600 lbs.: the amount of CO_2 released into the atmosphere by a single 5.5-pound shortboard during its life cycle (creation of blank, glue, resins and other components; manufacture; repairs; disposal). Multiply this by 400,000 to get an idea of how much CO_2—a greenhouse gas—is being added to the atmosphere annually by this one surf-related product.
- Millions: number of fins and fin plugs made each year, using toxic polyester resins and petroleum-based plastics.
- 250 tons: amount of neoprene (petroleum-based synthetic) from wetsuits that is thrown away each year. Wetsuit manufacture involves PVC and other toxic, non-biodegradable chemicals.
- 6,000,000: number of bars of surf wax used every year. Most surf wax includes high percentages of petroleum by-products and other toxic, non-biodegradable compounds.
- 6,000 tons: amount of sunscreen that is added to the ocean each year. Most sunscreens contain chemicals that, among other effects, bleach and kill coral. Ironically, some ingredients in sunscreens have been linked to cell damage and hormone disruption in users.

Do you really love me, or are you just using me?

There are no quick and easy solutions, but if we all seek out the least toxic products and use them well (make that old board or wetsuit last another year or two), we can try to make a difference.

PART III: KNOW YOUR BREAK

What's it like at low tide?

Do your homework

You're on a roll. You've been working out and you've read up on waves and how they are formed. You understand the difference between long-period and short-period swell; you know what Southern Hemi means to surfers. Time to hit the water!

Or not.

You may need to do a little on-site recon, just as serious people do in other sports. When playing "away" games, NFL coaches walk the field before each game. They check the location of game and play clocks, the condition of the playing surface, wind conditions at ground level, and other factors that could affect the outcome of the game. Ski racers aren't allowed to ski the course before a race, but they can and do sideslip the hill outside the gates, making mental notes of gate placement, bumps, flat spots, snow conditions, and other variables. Golfers try to play at least a round or two on the same course before a tournament, to observe everything they can. During play, they may walk dozens of yards from their ball, in the direction of the green, to double check terrain and conditions, before going back to the ball and making their shot.

Yet some surfers will attempt to surf a break with no idea of what it's like. They don't know the bottom, they don't know what swell or tide works best, they have no idea of how the waves break. They just show up and hope to have a good session. This isn't as bad a diving into a pool without checking to see if there's water in it, but sometimes it's a close second.

Now, we know you're not one of these hapless types, but you've probably seen them from time to time. So just for a moment, imagine what you'd experience if you were...

One of your friends has started surfing a different break, and you want to try it yourself. For some reason he never seems to have time to take you there and show you the ropes, so you decide to go it alone. After all, you've been surfing for a few years; how hard can it be?

When you get there, you see surfers in the water. But there doesn't seem to be any way to get down to the beach. There are some surfer-dude types sitting on a bench, but when you ask them, they give you some sort of sarcastic answer. So you go back to your car, get out your cell phone, and call your surf pal to ask him. When you hang up, you notice a couple of guys giving you stink-eye.

Well, maybe they're just hung over. You wax up, put on your leash, and head for the top of the cliff. On the way, your leash gets caught on a bush. As you untangle it, you hear the surfer-dude types snickering. What's with these guys?

Following your buddy's instructions, you find the path to the beach, being careful not to trip over your leash. You paddle out. On the way out, you hit your fin on a submerged rock, but there doesn't seem to be any damage.

Everyone is sitting in a fairly tight pack, but there's another spot nearby where the swells seem to be humping up pretty well, so you set up there. Why be a sheep? Be your own man! A set comes. You paddle for the first wave but it rolls right on past. You try the next wave with the same result. After a couple more sets like these you give up and join the rest of the group. They don't seem especially friendly, but you didn't come here to make friends, you came here to surf! And you know the rules: don't paddle around people, don't drop in, yield the right-of-way to a surfer who's already on the wave.

The first set moves a lot of people out of the lineup as they catch waves. It's a long set, and it's quickly followed by another. By the middle of the second set, most of the other surfers have either caught a wave or been caught inside. Most people seem to be going left, but you don't like to go left—it's backside for you and you don't like to surf backside. You'll go right and have it all to yourself.

You paddle for the next wave. Remembering the frustration you just experienced at the other peak, you start early to be sure to catch the wave, paddling straight for shore to maximize your chances. There's a guy paddling out inside, but you're sure you'll get past him with no problem.

Suddenly there's a violent swirl and surge of water directly in front of you. Just as you feel the tail of your board rising, lifted by the swell, the wave jacks up. You never get to your feet; halfway up and you're pitched straight toward the beach, then body-slammed and bounced off the reef. As you finally come to the surface and reel in your board, the guy who was paddling out snarls something unprintable, directed at you. OK, so he was closer than you thought. Is it your fault the wave caught you by surprise?

You end up getting a couple of rides, but the vibes are bad and you never really get a chance to show them what you can do. On your last wave, you hit your fin again, this time on a rock that didn't seem to be there earlier. You paddle out of the impact zone and into a channel to go in. Getting out was easy, but for some reason paddling in is twice as hard. You really have to work at it to get to the beach.

As you come out of the water, your leash wraps around your feet and you fall down in the shorebreak. When you slog up the path and reach the top of the bluff, the surfer-dude types are openly laughing. What, they never had an off-day? Later, when you ask your friend why he didn't warn you about all this, he shrugs and says he didn't have any problems. What went wrong?

Macro Factor: Swell Direction

A big part of ocean knowledge is an understanding of swell direction and how it affects the breaks you want to ride. Let's begin with a refresher on compass headings.

As shown on the compass rose below, by convention north is shown as "up" on maps and charts, and the compass is divided into 360 degrees, starting at the top (north) and increasing clockwise (to the right) as you move around the circle.

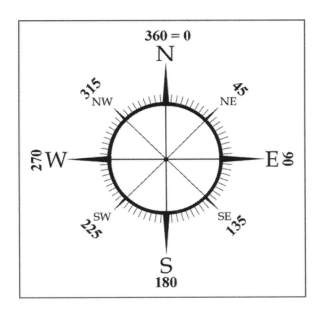

Compass Rose

FACTOID: COMPASS ROSE

The compass rose is so called because early versions were elaborate drawings resembling the petals of a rose.

Compasses are magnetic, and the compass needle orients itself to the earth's magnetic field. The problem is that true north (the North Pole, the northern end of the axis around which the earth rotates) is not the same as magnetic north (north as shown by a compass). In addition, the difference between true north and magnetic north is not constant, but depends on where you are located on the planet.

Swell direction from buoys and surf reports is stated in terms of true north, so even if you take a compass to the beach to check the orientation of your favorite break, your reading will not tell you exactly which way the coast faces relative to the swell. But a general idea is much better than no idea at all, and if you're serious about understanding the orientation of your break, it's well worth it to pick up a small pocket compass at your local hardware store and keep it in your car. At some beaches, you'll be amazed at how different the orientation is from what you thought it was.

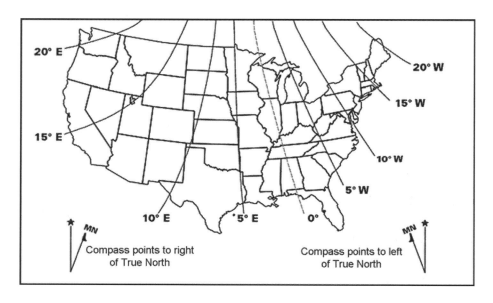

Magnetic Compass: Deviation from True North

FACTOID: WHY 360°?

Why are there 360 degrees in a circle, and in the compass? Wouldn't it be simpler to have a nice, round number like 100, or 1000? Or a cleaner multiple of 100, like 400 (easy to divide in quadrants)?

The answer lies in the length of a year. The ancients realized that there was some sort of circular or cyclical motion involving the sun and the earth, resulting in seasons that repeated in a pattern every year, every certain number of days. Although their measurements weren't precise, they came pretty close when they calculated approximately 360 days in a year. They knew that this wasn't exactly right, so they took care of the deviation by adding a few days "off-calendar," usually some sort of magical or religious period where the days had a special quality. And the 360-day year may have helped them to simplify the math of the circle, especially in the centuries before the invention of the decimal point.

How does swell direction affect your break?

Simple. The way the waves break will depend on the angle at which the swell strikes the bottom. Some angles will create long, peeling walls and barrels. The same size and period swell at a different angle can create anything from unmakeable closeout waves to mushy shoulders. And at certain angles, the result may be no surf at all. Let's look at the details.

You may hear some surfers mention the "magic number" for swell. What does this mean?

No matter where you surf, some swells will fail to produce surf at your break because they will fail to reach the shore. Take a look at the map on the next page, an unusual-shaped point of land with a compass rose superimposed on it. The darker area is the ocean.

Clearly, no matter what the swell direction, it's going to hit someplace on the peninsula, and probably on one of the beaches above and below the peninsula's base. But what about the magic number?

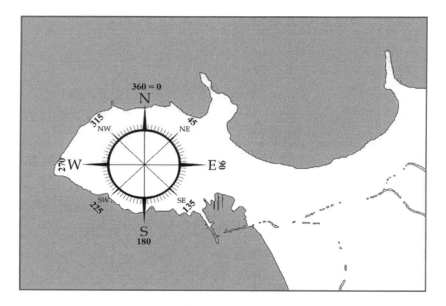

Obviously waves coming from the north, for example, will be unable to reach the south side of the peninsula, so any swell from 360° will fail to produce waves on the south side. As you move around the peninsula (and compass) in a counterclockwise direction, at some point the swell angle to the south-facing beach will be such that waves can create surf on the south shore. This compass reading is sometimes called the magic number—the maximum (or minimum) swell angle required to produce surf on a given beach.

Since the angle required depends on the depth and configuration of the ocean floor, there is no way to predict the exact magic number by simply looking at the map—the only way to do this is through observation—but you can get a good approximation and refine it as you correlate buoy readings with actual events in the surf zone.

The surf, of course, will depend on the bottom configuration. If the entire area consists of rocky cliffs plunging straight down below the sea, forget about surfing and bring a mask and snorkel instead. But the beach above the base of the peninsula--a long, gradual curve tipped by points on both ends—has the look of an expanse of sand or cobbles, not craggy boulders.

The peninsula itself has a highly irregular shoreline, which may be indicative of a steep, rocky coast (erosion of softer soils tends to create smoother shorelines). But often along the shore of a rugged coast there are reefs, or sand or cobble deltas created by streams and rivers, with beautiful waves.

There appears to be a port or harbor facility (jetties and breakwaters) below the base of the peninsula (the south-east corner). Since most harbors require relatively deep water and a relatively sheltered location, we can guess that the south-east corner drops off fairly fast and is situated away from the biggest storms and swell. This doesn't mean that there is no surf nearby—but it does provide some clues.

The map also tells us that any swell from the north (anywhere from NE to NW) should hit the large bay above the base of the peninsula. At the same time, the curving points at either end of the bay may cause backwash, cross-swells and currents, especially on bigger days. Again, the only way to know for sure is to observe, but the map gives at least an indication. You can get more information online, where you can quickly find satellite or high-altitude imagery that will show you what the beach and reefs are like and—even in the absence of real-time surf cams—may give an idea of how the waves break there.

Getting back to your area: to learn what swells will create what types of conditions at various breaks, get in the habit of checking buoy readings for swell size and direction, then observing conditions at the beach. Before long a simple glance at the buoys will tell you which spots are likely to be good.

Macro Factor: Tides

Together with the swell and swell angle, the tide (high, low, rising, falling, slack) is the greatest ocean-related variable determining the size and characteristics of surf. This is obvious on the U.S. West Coast, where the difference in water depth between the highest high and the lowest low may often be seven or eight feet. Even in Hawai'i, where maximum tidal depth differences are often less than two feet, there's an amazing difference between surfing a break at low tide and the same break at a higher tide.

It's easy to find out the tides for the day. Surf shops, dive shops and other places have pocket-sized tide tables for the entire year. The tides appear in the weather section of the newspaper. And you can find tide tables online. You might even buy a watch with built-in tidal information. And yet many people show up to surf without the slightest notion of what the tide is doing, even though knowing can make the difference between a great session and a waste of time.

Tides are much more than a simple sloshing to and fro of the world's oceans, created by the gravitational attraction of the moon. Tides are caused by a complicated set of factors including the sun, the moon, the earth's rotation, the configuration of coastline and sea floor, atmospheric pressure, wind, currents and other forces. While some of these (such as the action of the sun and the moon, or the shape of the coast and sea floor) lend themselves to accurate long-term forecasting, others do not.

The complexity of the forces and factors that determine the tides creates some very counter-intuitive situations. For example, tidal changes in the Mediterranean are minimal—often less than one foot and in some areas zero. That's right, no tidal movement whatsoever. This would seem impossible: the water in a relatively small system should flow from one area to another in response to any rise and fall in level anywhere in the system. But it doesn't. So in the

Mediterranean there are areas of zero tidal change (amphidromic points) coexisting with areas like the Gulf of Gabes off the coast of Tunisia, which has a tidal range of nearly two meters (over six feet).

In addition, tides in the Atlantic Ocean have a significant effect on tides in the Strait of Gibraltar, but this effect declines rapidly once inside the Mediterranean itself.   One might think that simple hydraulics would cause these larger flows to affect all areas in a contiguous body of water (as the tidal ebb and flow of the Pacific Ocean creates massive changes and currents throughout bodies of water like San Francisco Bay or the Atlantic does in the Bay of Fundy), and yet they don't.

FACTOID: TIDAL FLOW

The Bay of Fundy, in Nova Scotia, has the highest tides in the world. With every tidal cycle 100 billion tons of water—more than the flow of all the world's freshwater rivers combined—flow in and out of the bay. These massive tidal surges range in depth from 11 feet to an astounding 53 feet.

The tidal cycle

Tide tables are not guarantees, but estimated predictions.   The science involved is incredibly complicated (one oceanographer says it makes nuclear physics look very straightforward by comparison) and the forecasts are not totally accurate.   While generally very close to observed measurements, at times they may be off by as much as ten percent or more.   The discrepancy shown in the graph on the following page is greater than most, but it illustrates the possibility of error.   For surf purposes, this degree of difference won't usually matter.

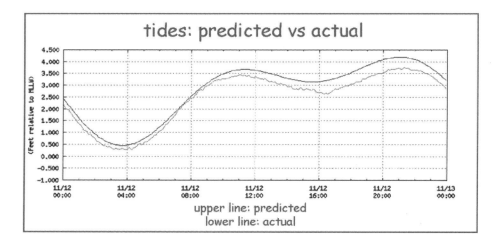

tides: predicted vs actual

upper line: predicted
lower line: actual

Another variable is the interval between tides. We often think of the tides as rising and falling in a nice, even pattern: high, low, high, low, roughly six hours apart, with the entire cycle occurring about half an hour later each day. And in fact, there are usually four tidal extremes (two high tides and two low tides) in every 24-hour period. This is depicted in nice, regular tidal curves:

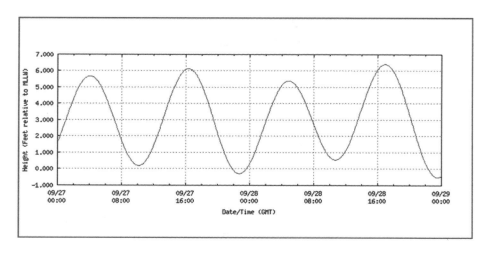

If only things were always that simple! But because of the irregularity of tidal oscillation, the regular, symmetrical curve becomes increasingly distorted, as shown in the following graph.

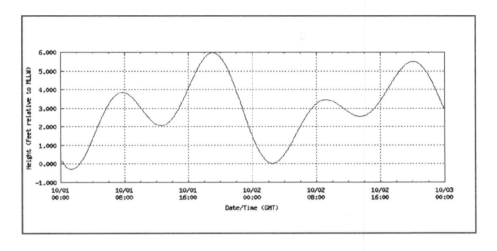

Eventually (see next page), one of the highs or lows is the same as its neighbor, blending the two extremes into one. The result is a 24-hour period with only three extremes instead of the expected four. Depending on the location, this may occur about every 5-8 days throughout the year. Less common (as few as a couple of times per year) are days with only two tidal extremes. And occasionally (only once a year in some locations) there are days in which there is only one tidal extreme. Keep in mind that tidal activity at every location— even spots quite close to each other—is different, due to the extreme complexity of the forces and factors that determine tidal times and flows.

If you're serious about surfing a different break, make a point of checking it out at an extreme low (preferably a minus) tide. You may be surprised at what you see: jagged reefs that weren't even hinted at when you looked at it a few hours earlier. Not every rock or reef reveals itself with a boil—it all depends on the bottom configuration. The best way to know is to observe at low tide. In addition to looking for hidden hazards, try to imagine how different swell directions might break on different parts of a reef or point. What angle will create waves that break best for surfing?

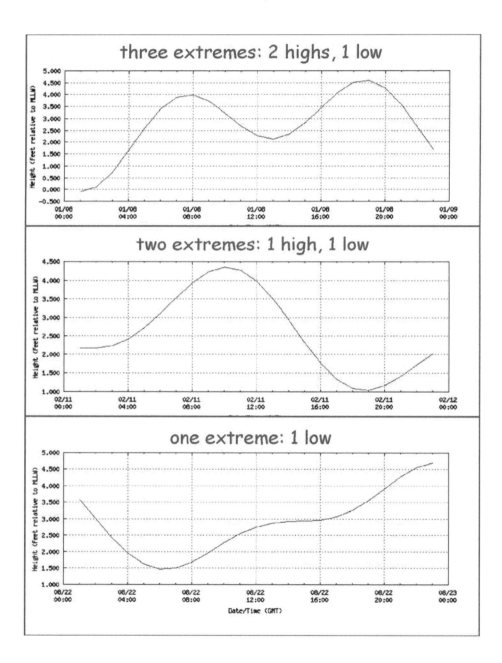

What tide is best for surfing?

Not surprisingly, the answer is "it depends." In general, most breaks work better at a medium tide. Extreme low tides tend to degrade the form of waves, and at many breaks the surf simply shuts down at low tide. High tides, on the other hand, put so much water depth on top of the reefs and bars where surf is normally found that waves keep on rolling and refuse to break. In addition, at many breaks—especially where there are cliffs or a steep shoreline, very high tides create backwash that makes waves back off and fill in.

But for every rule, there are exceptions. Some breaks actually work better at high tide, and there are breaks where the high-tide backwash adds to the fun. When hit by backwash, an incoming wave can jack up much higher and faster than a normal wave, creating a more challenging ride (for an example, see the cover illustration of this book.) Even breaks that normally require a medium (in Southern California, about 2-3 foot) tide, can be outstanding on higher tides if the swell direction is right. And low tide can also be an asset: at spots where low tide ruins the normal lineup, different, unusual and rideable breaks may start to work nearby when the tide is low. Finally, changes in swell size and direction can make a major difference in the way a given surf spot holds up under higher or lower tides.

The only way to know for sure how any given break will work at any given tide is by observation. Take some time to check out your favorite spots at various tidal depths. You might be surprised at what you see.

How about incoming tide as opposed to outgoing? In general, an incoming tide will give the waves more push and thickness, which means more power. An outgoing tide may reduce the speed and power of the waves, but often makes them more hollow. One disadvantage of an outgoing tide is that it tends to reinforce any rip currents that may be operating. These, in turn, will tend to degrade the surf in their immediate area. The effect of the tide is heavily influenced by the flow. If the high tide is, say, 6 feet, and the low is a minus 0.5, the water will recede at about one foot per hour (based on a typical time of about 6 hours between a high and a low). This will generate an incredible amount of energy going against the energy of the incoming waves.

Finally, there's the issue of slack tide. As the tide reaches a high (or low) and turns to flow in the opposite direction, there is a period of little or no tidal motion. At most breaks, this corresponds to a decrease in wave activity—i.e., the surf decreases or shuts down. This condition lasts for up to an hour at many breaks. Again, the best way to find out how your beach behaves is to observe it under different conditions.

FACTOIDS: SEA LEVEL

- *In Southern California the highest high tide of each day is followed by the lowest low tide. What's the pattern in your area?*
- *We tend to think of water as non-compressible but in reality, due to the immense pressure created by the weight of the thousands of feet of water depth in the oceans, the water is compressed. If the water in the ocean somehow became totally non-compressible, the level of the Pacific Ocean would be 150 feet higher than it is today. Even the pressure of the atmosphere has an effect, although much smaller: in the absence of atmospheric pressure, the surface of the Pacific would rise over half a foot.*
- *In a non-El Niño year the level of the Western Pacific is about two feet higher than it is during an El Niño year.*
- *Average ocean levels worldwide have risen over 4 inches since 1950, and the rate is increasing. Even a small depth change can have a noticeable effect on a surf break.*

Obstacles to Wave Action

If the ocean were an unbroken expanse of open water, predicting surf at your break would be a lot easier. But there are islands out there, and they can have a major effect on surf.

Wave Refraction

Surface waves can be bent (refracted). When surfers say that a swell "wraps" they mean that it is being bent (usually around a point) so that it travels in a different direction, orienting itself more perpendicular to the shoreline and generating surf. This bending or "wrapping" increases the swell window at breaks where swells are blocked by the contours of the land.

As the swell approaches a point of land at an angle, the shallow water off the tip of the point exerts drag on the base of each wave nearest the shore, causing that part of the wave to slow down. The rest of the wave, still in deeper water, continues at full speed. The effect is like grabbing the outstretched arm of someone who is running past you: the arm slows down, the body keeps moving, and the person is dragged in a circular motion. (In some places you can observe a complete reversal of direction, as a wave wraps all the way around a sand spit and heads back in the opposite direction on the other side of the spit.) The size and power of a wrapping wave are reduced as energy is absorbed by the sea floor.

When a swell wraps, it tends to reduce disorganization in mixed swells. So on mixed-swell days, a break that is the result of wrapping may have waves which, although smaller, are cleaner than the waves at more exposed beaches.

Refraction also occurs in bays or inlets. The water closest to the center of the bay is deeper. As a wave approaches the bay, the shallower bottom near the edges of the bay begins to exert drag on the base of the wave as it passes over, causing the ends of the wave to slow down. The part of the wave that is nearer the center of the bay continues at its original speed, bending the wave into a curve.

Refraction may also be created by sandbars, submerged reefs, submarine canyons, and other irregularities in the ocean floor. At such locations, the waves may be much larger than they are in a spot just a few dozen yards away. Waves formed by refraction of this type often take the form of a bowl, in which the wave energy is focused toward the center of the bowl. These waves can jack much faster and break much harder than a straight wall of the same size.

FACTOID: REEF AND ISLAND WRAP AND RE-FOCUS

Waves can wrap all the way around an island which is less than 2-3 wave lengths wide. A larger island causes a wave shadow zone, but at some point to the lee of the island continuing refraction may focus the wave energy from two directions, creating very powerful—and disorganized—waves.

Underwater reefs and sandbars can have the same effect. At some bowl-type breaks (created by underwater refraction of the wave base), waves that start in a bowl configuration go on to form an X as the wave energy wraps around the submerged reef and then runs into itself in a crossing pattern between the reef and the shore. Riding these waves can be a challenge, but it's fun if you're prepared for it.

Island Wave Shadows

Let's take a closer look at islands and the effect they have on swell. In the map on the following page (which shows the Southern California coast from Point Conception to Mexico), the light areas are land, the dark gray areas are ocean, and the black areas are wave shadows caused by islands and points of land blocking the swell. Small white areas indicate areas of higher swell and surf. The map shows a small day (0.8ft at 8-second intervals; 1.8ft at 11-second intervals), but on larger days the principle is the same: islands and points of land block the swells in leeward locations.

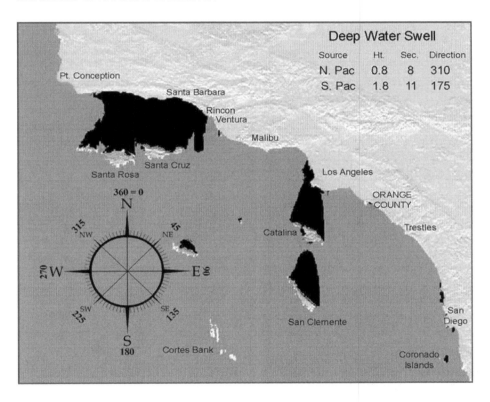

Deep Water Swell			
Source	Ht.	Sec.	Direction
N. Pac	0.8	8	310
S. Pac	1.8	11	175

Island wave shadows block the swell

Details: on a south swell, the entire area around Santa Barbara is surfless; the first break to the south is in the vicinity of Rincon (north of Ventura). Notice also that wave shadows can be created by points of land, as they are near San Diego in this image. The best Southern California breaks for this swell direction are places like Malibu and Orange County. Would a swell from this direction hit your area?

What about the very small NW swell were coming from 310°? Point Conception should effectively block this swell from hitting most of the mainland area shown. In addition, for most of the area north of San Diego the swell angle is almost parallel to the coast and therefore unlikely to produce good surf even if this swell were bigger.

FACTOID: OFFSHORE SURFING

Cortes Bank (near the bottom of the map) is a very shallow chain of undersea mountains in water half a mile deep about 115 miles west of San Diego. On the right swell, it produces monster waves that can be ridden. This was attempted, probably for the first time (beware of any absolute claim of a "first"), about 1960 by Jim Fisher, an incredible waterman who would go for almost anything when it came to waves. But trying to paddle into waves of up to 40 feet, over 100 miles from land, nothing to line up on, no leash, no wetsuit, and no nearby backup (the boat that brought him wisely stayed well away from the break) proved to be too much even for Fisher.

The Effects of Wind

Wind not only creates waves, it affects them throughout their lifetime. From ripples to whitecaps, winds in the surf zone can cause dramatic changes in surf size and quality. Points to remember:
- Air moves from high pressure areas to low pressure areas, creating wind.
- In the Northern Hemisphere, the air in high pressure areas moves in a clockwise direction; in lows it rotates counterclockwise. (In the Southern Hemisphere, the directions are reversed.) For surfers in Southern California, for example, this means that a high over Nevada can create offshore winds in the surf zone.
- Wind patterns are highly variable. In only a few miles of coastline, the wind can be a stiff offshore in one spot, dead calm in another, and howling onshore in a third.

- Wind, like water, flows around obstacles, changing the surf in the process. On O'ahu, for example, the same Trade Winds that create an offshore at Waikiki make powerful side-shore chop below Diamond Head as they flow around the mountain.
- Canyons act as wind corridors that focus and intensify wind.
- In an offshore wind, you need to take extra strokes on takeoff; pop up low and crouch forward, as you would when making a late takeoff.
- When surfing in a crosswind, you'll go slower—and have a rougher ride—when going against the wind. You'll need to stay low, just as you would in an offshore.

Wave Changes in Shallow Water

Now we're getting into an area of prime concern to surfers. That beautiful, long-period Southern Hemi swell or big South Atlantic swell is getting close to shore. But will it produce epic waves?

Earlier we noted that deep-water waves are unaffected by the configuration of the sea floor, since in mid-ocean the base of the wave—even if hundreds of feet deep—is nowhere near the bottom of the sea. But when waves enter shallow water (which, as you recall, is defined as water that is less than ½ the wavelength) they encounter enough resistance to change their behavior.

When waves approach the shore, the decreasing ocean depth causes them to slow down. At the same time, their height increases and they change shape: symmetrical sine curves morph into sharper peaks and flatter valleys as the wave crests become shorter compared to the troughs between waves. The period (frequency) stays the same, but the wavelength gets shorter (i.e., the waves bunch up, getting closer together). Individual waves stop leapfrogging and disappearing (as they did in deep water) and keep their place in the wave train, which is now a visible set.

When the water depth is less than 1.3 times the wave's height, the wave breaks. (Remember that the height of the wave has been increasing as the base of the wave is affected by decreasing ocean depth.) The steeper the sea floor (i.e., the more abrupt the change in ocean depth), the quicker the wave will break. If the change in ocean depth is very abrupt, the wave will increase in height very quickly (in surfing terms, it jacks up or stands up) and the crest will often be thrown forward (the wave pitches or throws out). How much the wave will jack depends on the period and the steepness of the ocean floor. For example, one measured observation revealed that a 20-foot swell with a 21-second period could jack up to about 50 feet when it hit shallow water and broke.

To visualize this process, think of a pole-vaulter. The vaulter runs toward the bar, plants the pole in a small pit, and starts upward. The front end of the pole stops when it hits the pit. The vaulter's forward motion is converted into upward motion, hurling him upward and forward. If he has sufficient speed, his momentum will carry him up and over the bar, after which he falls forward and down. To continue the analogy, wave period is comparable to the length of the vaulter's pole: the longer the pole, the higher the possible vault—and the longer the period, the higher the wave when it jacks.

When a wave breaks, the crest of the wave is the vaulter and the pit is the reef, sandbank or other obstacle which impedes the forward progress of the wave. The base of the wave hits the reef, the water surges upward and forward as the wave jacks up, and the wave ends up breaking. A gently-sloping undersea contour acts as a brake on the incoming wave, which results in a weaker, smaller peak and break. (Imagine the pole-vaulter dragging the front of the pole in the dirt before planting it in the pit; his speed would be slowed and his potential vault would be lower.)

The biggest, quickest, hardest-breaking waves occur when the undersea contour is close to vertical. The base of the wave slams into the reef and comes to an abrupt stop, forcing the energy upward and hurling the column of water up and forward. The opposite happens if there is an underwater obstacle followed by a hole: like a pole-vaulter aborting his jump, the wave begins to jack up as it hits the reef or sandbank, but backs down again because the water column was not forced up enough to cause the wave to break. Each time this happens, the energy of the wave is decreased as energy is transmitted to the sea floor and refracted laterally.

Putting on the brakes

In the shallow water near the surf zone, wave speed is somewhat counter-intuitive. Since long-period waves travel so rapidly in the open sea compared to short-period waves, we might expect them to travel faster in shallow water as well. But in fact, waves of all periods "max out" to about the same speed in water shallower than about 60 feet. Even at ocean depths of 20 meters (about 66 feet) the speed of long-period waves is only very slightly higher than that of shorter-period waves. (At ocean depths greater than this, the difference in speed begins to increase more rapidly as you move to deeper water.)

If you think about it, this actually makes sense: the longer the period, the deeper the base of the wave. Therefore, longer-period waves start dragging on the sea floor earlier, which slows them down. By the time they reach the surf zone, their speed is the same as that of shorter-period waves.

The table on the next page shows how waves—regardless of period— are slowed to the same speed in shallow water. At sufficiently shallow depths there is a maximum wave speed for that depth, which is the same for all wave periods.

Equalization of Wave Speeds in Increasingly Shallow Water
(all figures are rounded approximations)

OCEAN DEPTH (approximate)	PERIOD (seconds) - SPEED		
	20 sec	**17 sec**	**12 sec**
Deep Water	70mph	60mph	42mph
200ft	55mph	50mph	42mph
100ft	40mph	37mph	35mph
66ft		30mph	
33ft		22mph	
16ft		16mph	
10ft		12mph	

What?!? You've ridden waves of all sizes, and you know from experience that big, long-period waves are faster! You've felt the speed difference yourself, many times. How can they be the same?

Like the "disappearing act" of deep-water waves and their super-speed relative to the wave train they're in, this is another aspect of ocean waves that is counter-intuitive. But this one has a simple and totally logical explanation.

Remember that long-period waves, being thicker than shorter-period waves, contain more energy. Even in shallow water, at any given speed they will provide more push and drive you forward more strongly than a smaller, shorter-period wave. As a result, your board is more responsive and you can generate more speed on turns.

And there's more: as waves move into shallower water, they increase in height. Because of their greater thickness and energy, long-period waves will get taller, and will jack up faster and higher when they hit a reef, as their forward motion is converted to vertical motion. This means that in general they are steeper, and you can drop down the face faster on a steep wave than you can on a flatter one.

There's also the speed of the water (as opposed to the speed of the wave). The quick redirection of the wave's energy means that water is driven up the face very rapidly, and the increased height of the wave means that water has to go farther—and travel faster—to get from the still-water level to the crest of the wave. Since you're surfing across and down the face, the increased speed of the water rushing up the wave translates into your totally accurate perception of increased speed relative to the water.

It's like airspeed vs. groundspeed in an airplane in a headwind, or absolute vs. relative speed when water-skiing or wakeboarding behind a boat going upriver. If the river is flowing at, say, 15mph and the boat's water speed indicator reads 30mph, the speed of the boat (and the person behind it) is 30mph relative to the water, but only 15mph relative to the shore.

And of course there's the question of distance traveled: since you're not going straight off, but at an angle, you're going farther in the same amount of time. In other words, you're going faster than the wave, and each turn and cutback adds to the distance traveled. Longer distance in equal time means higher speed. So when surfing a big, long-period wave you can be flying across the face—and over the water rushing up the face—at high speed, but your speed directly toward the beach is far slower.

Finally, there's the issue of wind. As waves move forward, they push against air. This creates relative wind: the difference in speed between the moving wave and the air. Moreover, the air has to move out of the way of the wave, and it does so by flowing up the face of the wave and over the top. This creates an airflow: even on a still day, there's a breeze blowing up the face of each wave. The higher the wave, the farther the air has to go—and the faster it has to move—to get up the face and out of the way. So the higher the wave, the faster the apparent wind it generates, which adds to the sensation of speed.

Reduced Speed Zone

The waves in the above image are coming ashore in big, long-period sets, but at this depth their forward speed would be the same even if their wave period were only half as long. Breaking on a steep reef in about 12 to 15 feet of water, they jack up quickly and they have plenty of power, with water rushing up the face at high speed.

This picture was taken from about 25 feet above sea level; above the top of the second wave in the set you can just make out the top of the third wave, which is almost blocked from view.

Interpreting Swell Information

What does the following surf forecast for Orange County, CA, tell you? The swell is supposed to be four feet. This should make some decent waves—or should it? Use the map on page 57 to decide.

SURF ZONE FORECAST
ORANGE COUNTY, CA, COASTAL AREAS-

OUTLOOK FOR THURSDAY...1 TO 2 FEET.
WEST SWELL 4 FEET AT 6 SECONDS FROM 286 DEGREES.
SOUTH SWELL 2 FEET AT 16 SECONDS FROM 222 DEGREES.

There are three main items to look for:
1. Size of swell
2. Swell period
3. Swell direction

Right away you notice what seems to be a discrepancy. There's supposed to be a 4-foot west swell, plus a 2-foot south, but the forecast calls for surf of only 1 to 2 feet. Why is the surf predicted to be so small?

A big part of the answer is in the period. The 4-foot west has an interval (period) of only 6 seconds. This very short period indicates a weak, almost choppy wind swell. Short period = low energy = small, weak waves.

In addition, 286° is actually not west (270°), but higher up on the compass. Much of this swell will be blocked by the northern Channel Islands and the point of land near L.A., and what gets through will be too parallel to the shore. Furthermore, you know that short-period swell isn't very deep (the base of the waves doesn't extend very far down below the surface of the ocean), which means that this 6-

second swell won't wrap except in very shallow water. So what little of it arrives at the beach will be small and weak.

How about the south swell? It's only 2 feet, but at 16 seconds it should have decent strength due to the increased energy contained in its deeper, broader wave form. You'd think it would generate some fun waves in the waist-high range, maybe even better. Part of the problem may be interference from the west swell. As the short-period 4-foot waves collide with the 2-foot south swell in shallow water, the energy in the latter is diminished.

Another factor may be the shadow of Catalina and/or San Clemente Island. A swell from 222° puts much of Orange County in the lee of one or both of these islands, so that the mainland breaks fall into the island swell shadow. And wave refraction from the islands will create disorganized wave patterns, degrading whatever swell does reach the mainland shore. Finally, various combinations of wind, currents and other factors can reduce the swell to the small size of the forecast.

How big is big?

A common question among surfers is "how big was it?" And you often hear predictions (or boasts) of wave sizes that defy common sense. As mentioned earlier, oceanographers measure the height of waves from trough to crest, either in feet or in meters. On the U.S. mainland, most surfers calculate the height of the face of the wave as somewhat less than this; the flatter portion of the wave near the bottom of the trough doesn't count. In Hawai'i, surfers discuss wave height in terms of the back of the wave. While this method may be more realistic in a certain sense (because it generally gives a more accurate description of the difference between the top of the wave and still-water level at that point), it can lead to extreme cognitive dissonance.

For example, "slab" waves, formed when a swell hits a certain type of reef, often are very flat on the backside, even though the face of the wave may be many feet tall. Slab waves are deep-water waves hitting a reef in such a way that the pre-wave outgoing surge drains considerable water depth off the reef; following this the onrushing deep-water wave doesn't increase in height, but essentially collapses into a hole in the ocean. In essence, these waves are all face and no back. So a violent, nasty wave with a 20-foot face might only have a 3-foot back. For waves like these, backside measurement does not provide a very accurate representation of the situation.

In addition, at some breaks you can see the backs of wave grow and shrink as they pass over reefs. You may even see waves that come toward the lineup, then keep growing as they pass under you and head for the shore, their height increasing as they reach shallower water. At which point do you estimate the size of the back of the wave? And of course you never see the back of the waves you catch.

One method of wave measurement that avoids reference to feet or meters is to measure the height of the wave face relative to the body height of a surfer: head high, overhead, double overhead, and so on. But even this can lead to absurd calculations. At one break on an overhead day, an eight-year old kid asked a surfer coming in, "How big was it out there?" The surfer, a tall, college-basketball type, stretched one arm up over his head to indicate the size. "Wow!" said the kid, "Triple overhead!" Well, yes, if you're only three feet tall.

Size isn't everything

Even if there's no argument about the height of the wave, size isn't the only thing that matters. You may recall the controversy that erupted a few years back in connection with the Billabong biggest wave of the year award. A surfer riding a break off the coast of France won with a 60-foot wave, amid sets judged to be 60 to 80 feet high. Immediately the complaining began. Critics said the wave was too soft, too easy to ride, not challenging enough. One surfer said he would let his 9-year-old son ride a wave like that with no worries. (The French surfers diplomatically declined to argue the issue, and reassured everyone that they fully recognized the great difficulty of other waves.)

The critics had a valid point. No matter what the size category of the wave—huge, large, or small—there's more to it than height alone.

Take a look at the comparison photos on the following page. The lower wave is a bit larger, but the upper wave is thicker, more vertical, and more powerful. The portion of the unbroken wave ahead of the surfer is steeper and "bowling" toward him, which will focus the energy when it breaks (much as a parabolic reflector focuses sound, light, heat and electromagnetic waves). You can see that the lip, which is much thicker, is pitching out farther. The lower wave is a straight, non-bowling face, so the energy isn't being focused as it is in the upper wave. There's no doubt that the upper wave, even though smaller, requires more skill to catch and ride and will create a more violent wipeout and longer hold-down if the surfer doesn't make the wave.

Sometimes this type of difference can be seen on a single wave. At some surf spots, the reefs further offshore have less abrupt slopes on the seaward side. This means that when set waves break, they jack up less rapidly and have less steep drops. After these waves break, as they move toward shore they encounter inshore reefs with steeper seaward slopes. When this happens, the unbroken part of the wave jacks up quickly and pitches out.

Riding a wave like this can be an interesting lesson in shallow-water-wave dynamics, as the wave you're on suddenly gets steeper—and your ride gets faster due to the increased velocity of water rushing up the face—as it passes over the inshore reef.

Size does matter, but...

Reef Boils

What's the message?

We mentioned reef boils briefly in the context of the takeoff. Now it's time to provide a bit more detail on what reef boils can do for you, as well as to you.

When underwater currents or wave action strike the steep faces of reefs or other obstacles, water surges upward in a churning motion. At the surface, this appears as a reef boil. Reef boils can be a great aid in surfing.

Since the presence of the boil indicates a reef, it stands to reason that waves should, at some point, break on that reef. In addition, if the reef is steep enough to create a large boil, it's likely that waves passing over it will jack up sharply and break with a lot of force. What does this mean to you as a surfer?

When taking off outside a boil, the boil indicates the point at which you need to have caught the wave, gotten up, and made your move (turn left or right). If you don't, you'll be at the mercy of the wave jacking up suddenly over the reef. Depending on the wave and the reef, you might free-fall as the face of the wave drops out from under you, or you might be pitched by the lip as it catapults forward. Either way, it won't be fun. It's like taking off in an airplane: the distance from your starting point to the boil is the length of the runway, and if you're not up before the end of the runway, you crash.

You may find that the waves are jacking up on an outside boil, but failing to break. This often happens on a higher tide, when a reef that normally would be breaking is a little too deep to do so. Sometimes you can use the boil—or rather, the quick jump made by the wave as it passes over the boil—to give you enough acceleration to catch the unbroken wave and ride it until it finally breaks further toward shore. This is easier on a longboard, of course, but shortboarders do it, too.

Finally, a reef boil or sand boil can be a good indicator, letting you know that a set is coming. On a big days a boil may suddenly become very active during a lull, long before there's any visible sign of an approaching set. The massive energy of a large, long-period wave train creates pulses beneath the surface far ahead of the main waves, and this energy causes the boil to surge and churn before the set arrives. This activity isn't a guarantee that a large set is coming (the boil could be caused by a smaller set or by refracted energy from another direction), but it does provide one more useful indicator of what to expect.

FACTOID: SAND BOILS

A sandy bottom resists downward and sideways movements but not upward movements. The sand is drawn upward by the motion of water particles above it as a wave of energy passes overhead.

Currents

Rip Current: What comes in must go out

The ocean is filled with all sorts of currents, from long-term global flows to transitory local conditions.

Prevailing currents are those which tend to exist over time and usually cover large areas. The Pacific Coast of Japan has the Black Current (Kuroshio), which flows from south to north. This current segues into the North Pacific Current, which in turn leads to the California Current running north to south along the West Coast of the United States. The Gulf Stream flows from south to north along the U.S. East Coast. And so on. In general, prevailing currents have less immediate effect on surf than more localized currents, but they play an important role in shaping coastlines through their continual action.

One of their effects is to move sand and sediment up or down the coast, depositing it on the lee side of points and capes.

Bays and major inlets create significant local currents as they fill and empty with the changing of the tides. These currents move sand and sediment in smaller areas, often producing rapid changes in bottom contour. On Ocean Beach south of San Francisco Bay, for example, surf breaks appear, shift and disappear quite rapidly due to sand being redistributed on the ocean floor, in part by flows from the Bay.

Big swell and surf can create very strong local currents. Any time that large waves pass over a shallow area, some of the energy is refracted or spilled off laterally. At many point breaks and reef breaks, on a big day the water pouring sideways off the relatively shallow water of the break will drag you along with it, forcing you to paddle constantly against it to stay in the same place relative to the shore. If you don't, you'll quickly drift out of the lineup.

At some breaks with heavy shorebreak you can use the current coming off a point to help you get out past the surf line in the absence of a channel. Enter the water on the point, staying on the down-current side, walk out as far as possible (up to your chest), and wait for a lull. If you paddle straight out, the strong sideways current will sweep you off the point on the down-current side as you move seaward by paddling. The resulting course should enable you to bypass and avoid the shorebreak on the beach below the point, and if your timing is right you'll be out to the side of the impact zone before the next set comes through.

Rip currents, the most localized and unstable currents, are caused mostly by swell and wave action. When waves break, they push water toward shore. Somehow that water has to get back out past the surf line (if it didn't, water levels would increase and flood everything on the beach). The water from the surf moves in, then flows sideways down the beach, and back out as soon as it encounters—or carves—a channel.

On a sand beach, this action can cause rapid formation and destruction of sand bars and holes, which means that surfers have to shift their position constantly in order to catch waves. On big days, the sideshore current can carve trenches which make it hard to get in and out of the water. On the way out, it's like having to cross a moat to storm the castle. There may be two layers of shorebreak, one close to shore and the other on the outside of the trench carved by the current. On the way back in to shore, you may find that the sideshore current has carved a trench right where you need to put your feet down to escape the shorebreak.

For surfers, rip currents can be useful. Since they flow out through channels, they often indicate the best route out through the surf. And the flow itself, although usually choppy, will help you get out past the surf line that much faster on a big day. In addition, if you do get caught by a set while paddling out in a rip current, the action of the current moving in opposition to the surf reduces the force of the waves and makes it easier for you to duck dive or roll through them. On the way in, they can be an obstacle; a strong rip is so fast and powerful that even a surfer paddling hard can barely move forward against the current.

Rip currents are easy to spot: streaks of foam, a flow of choppy water, or both. (For examples, look at the rip current images on the first and last pages of this section on currents.) Remember that rips can flow outward, parallel to the beach, or in any other direction. On big days at some breaks, rips will drag a loose board out beyond the lineup and then up or down the coast, sometimes releasing it into the break at another beach, where it will wash up on shore. In the pre-leash era a loose board would occasionally wash up on a beach where no one was surfing, with no clue as to where it had come from.

Rip current between breaks: one-way street?

PART IV: DRY LAND SURF SCHOOL

Your training should get you ready to ride

Why train for surfing?

Surfing is one of the few sports where a coach can't stand nearby giving you advice, or guide you through the motion like a golf instructor. Once you're moving on a wave, you're on your own. What's worse, if you make a mistake when surfing you have to wait for another wave—anywhere from a few minutes to half an hour—so you can try to correct it. You can't simply get up and try again, or tee up another ball. In surfing, there are no second serves, no mulligans, and no counterpart of the pitching machine or tennis machine or mechanical bull. And when the wave does arrive, you can't surf entirely at your own pace—the wave dictates. It's all or nothing.

And yet few surfers ever practice. Surfing has no driving ranges, no practice serves, no endless pitching of baseballs or throwing bullet football passes through a car tire hanging from a tree. No surfer's equivalent of shadow boxing or hitting the heavy bag.

Surfers often jog or run, they may do situps and pushups, sometimes they ride bicycles; they may even pump iron. But rarely do they actually practice moves they'll need, or work the specific muscle groups that they'll use in the water. Result: muscle memory doesn't get laid down as fast. Compare skiing: you start standing up; you can get the feel of the skis by walking around on flat ground; you can pick a gentle slope, slide down a bit, stop, think about it, try it again.

Then there's the time factor. At many breaks, an average ride lasts less than 60 seconds—and even on a good day, you're doing well to catch 10 waves an hour. That adds up to under 10 minutes of practice time for each hour spent on the water. Compare this to skiing or snowboarding: a skier or snowboarder going top to bottom is limited only by conditioning: how far can he/she go before the legs burn out. On a good hill, a single run might equal an entire day of surfing, in terms of time spent building muscle memory by actually doing the activity. One day on the slopes can provide the surfing equivalent of a weeks' practice on the water. In addition, skiers and snowboarders don't have to wait days or weeks for a decent swell. If there's snow (real or artificial), they can hit it every day—for days or weeks at a time. Quite a disparity.

So as a surfer, you're facing a very steep learning curve. The solution is to practice key moves in a controlled environment, just like athletes in other sports.

Hence, the need for a surf-specific training program—one that's both effective and surf-oriented. One that will give you not only strength and conditioning, but also flexibility, agility, and practice doing the things you actually do to catch and ride a wave. Your surfing training program has to be practical, it has to be simple and accessible, and it has to help you surf better. And it has to be one that you will actually do. Not for a couple of days, weeks, or months, but—in some form or other—for many, many years.

That's what the training exercises in this book are all about. They're all designed for surfing. They're practical, they're simple, and they offer total freedom: do one, do two, do a dozen. Take 30 seconds, take five minutes, put in half an hour (if you do, you'll know you've had a workout!). The choice is yours.

The key to training and staying fit is largely habit. If you keep some small (maximum 3 pounds, to avoid wear and tear on joints) weights handy and get in the habit of doing an exercise or two during TV commercial breaks or while waiting for the toast to come up, you'll start looking forward to it. Eventually, you won't feel right unless you do an exercise (or two, or a dozen) every morning. It's like surfing as opposed to not surfing—the more you do it, the more you want to do it.

How to get the best results

KEY POINTS

- Weight limit 3 pounds per hand. Your muscles can do more, but over time you'll wear out your joints. Make up for light weight with more repetitions, which is more relevant for most activities, and especially for surfing. In addition, smooth low-resistance motion helps lubricate your joints.
- Don't rush or push yourself. Keep a firm, smooth, relaxed pace. Go at whatever speed feels natural on that day.
- If something hurts, don't do it. Pain is nature's way of telling you to do something else.

WHEN DOING AN EXERCISE FOR THE FIRST TIME

1. Do the motion with no weights, just empty hands, until it feels natural and comfortable. Then try it with the weights.
2. When you start with weights, do no more than 10 repetitions of any motion on the first day. Increase the number by up to 50% each day (10, 15, 20, 30, etc.) until you are doing as many as you decide is enough.
3. If you have to lay off due to injury or illness, follow step 2 above. Start with very few repetitions and build up gradually.

TIPS FOR A BETTER SESSION

Don't race the clock or try for personal bests. This isn't a contest, it's an opportunity to get in touch with your own body. Feel your muscles and tendons and joints working. Do some reps with your eyes closed and feel the pull of gravity and the pressure on your hands or feet against the floor. Become aware of your spatial orientation. All this is useful if you're free-falling through the whitewater of a breaking wave. Where are your feet, where's the board, which way is up? Make the answers second nature on dry land, and you'll do a lot better in the water.

Keep your training balanced. If you exercise the front, exercise the back; if you do something on the left, do it on the right; if you work the arms, work the legs.

Don't forget to stretch. If you start to tighten up during a workout, switch to a stretching exercise, then return to the exercise you were doing.

Pay attention to your breathing. In general—and especially if doing high-output actions (like popping up)—it's best to exhale on the exertion. But with lighter repetitive actions (such as paddling), to do this would be pointless; you'd be panting like a sled dog. Set up a rhythm to your breathing. On curls or reverse curls or paddling exercises, you might inhale two and exhale four. The same breathing rhythm might work for hip lifts using both legs. On single-leg hip lifts, which are twice as demanding, you'll want to breath faster, maybe one count in and two counts out. Whatever works for you. The point is to be aware of your breathing, and get into a rhythm.

PLEASE NOTE

- Each exercise is numbered (#1 through #36) only for convenient reference. The numbers do NOT indicate a sequence to follow.
- Each exercise is independent and can be done separately or with any other exercise or exercises. However, you are advised to always start with something undemanding before doing something more energetic.
- When in doubt, stretch first.

Section 1: Stretching and Flexibility

You need flexibility for high-impact situations

#1: Leg Stretch – Reach with One Hand

BENEFITS: Stretches hamstrings; also engages foot, upper body and neck. Keeping your hamstrings stretched not only helps avoid muscle pulls and tears, it also reduces strain on your lower back.

COMBINE WITH: Makes a nice warmup for #2 (Leg Stretch, Two Hands), and for Hip Lifts (#18, #19).

HOW TO DO IT:
Sit on the floor with legs extended. Cross one ankle over the other. The leg you are stretching is the lower leg; the leg that is crossed on top just lies there. Try to keep your lower back straight; the straighter your back, the more you stretch the leg.

Version (a): Reach forward to hold LOWER foot with opposite hand. (If RIGHT foot is the lower foot, hold it with the LEFT hand.)

Version (b): Reach forward to hold LOWER foot with hand on same side (RIGHT hand to RIGHT foot, or LEFT hand to LEFT foot). You will feel a very different pull on your body.

Both versions: use the muscles in lower leg to press back of knee to floor. Repeat this action 5-10 times in each position (looking front, looking right, looking left). Instead of just touching your toes, try to stretch them back. If you can, reach over your toes, grip the ball of your foot, and pull to stretch the plantar area and ankle.

TIPS: Stretch one leg, then lie back and do the Turtle (#22), then sit back up and do the other leg. When finished, lie back and then Pop up using Twisting Pop-up (#17).

a: L hand R foot

look front

look R

look L

#1

b: R hand R foot

look front

look R

look L

#2: Leg Stretch – Reach with Both Hands

BENEFITS: Stretches hamstrings; also engages foot, upper body and neck. A bilateral version of #1, to keep your hamstrings stretched and help reduce strain on your lower back.

COMBINE WITH: A good follow-up to #1 (Leg Stretch, One Hand); a good warmup for Hip Lifts (#18, #19).

HOW TO DO IT:
Sit on the floor with legs extended. Try to keep your lower back straight; the straighter your back, the more you stretch the leg.

- Version (a): Cross one ankle over the other. The leg you are stretching is the lower leg; the leg that is crossed on top just lies there. Reach forward to hold LOWER foot with both hands.
- Version (b): Keep legs parallel. Reach forward to hold one foot with each hand.
- Version (c): Spread legs slightly; hold one foot with each hand. Some people find version (c) easier than (b).

All versions: use leg muscles to press back of knees to floor. Repeat this action 5-10 times in each position (looking front, looking right, looking left). Instead of just touching your toes, try to stretch them back. If you can, reach over your toes, grip the ball of your foot, and pull to stretch the plantar area and ankle.

TIPS: Stretch, then lie back and do the Turtle (#22), then sit back up and stretch again. When finished, lie back and then Pop up using Twisting Pop-up (#17).

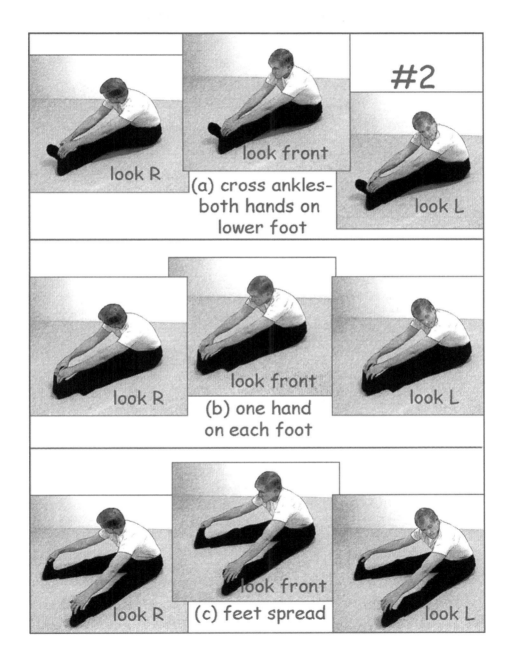

look R

look front

#2

(a) cross ankles–
both hands on
lower foot

look L

look R

look front

(b) one hand
on each foot

look L

look R

look front

(c) feet spread

look L

#3: Four-point Stretch

BENEFITS: Stretches back and inside of legs, while giving some exercise to the arms, shoulders and legs. A good 30-second Quickie exercise.

COMBINE WITH: A good warmup for Knee Thrusts (#24, #25) or Pop-up from Knees (#11). A "quickie" version of other leg stretches.

HOW TO DO IT:
- Put your feet about 2 shoulder widths apart, feet parallel.
- Keep knees straight but not locked and lean forward to rest your hands on the floor (Position 1).
- Still in Position 1, shift your weight slightly to the rear, ease off, and shift to the rear again. You should feel some gentle stretching in the back of your legs and connected areas. Repeat 10-12 times.
- Next, shift your weight to the right leg and bend your right knee slightly, keeping your left leg straight but not locked (Position 2). You should feel some gentle stretching in the inside of your left (straighter) leg. Push your weight gently in this direction, then ease off. Repeat 10-12 times.
- Now do the same thing on the other side, shifting your weight to the left leg and bending your left knee slightly, keeping your right leg straight but not locked (Position 3). Gently push and ease off, repeating 10-12 times.
- Finally, return to Position 1 and gently stretch a couple of times for bilateral symmetry.

TIPS: Don't get violent, just shift your weight gently in the desired direction. Don't strain anything on stretches. If one leg doesn't want to stretch as much as the other, don't force it.   Do NOT switch repeatedly from side to side; it's hard on your hips and knees.

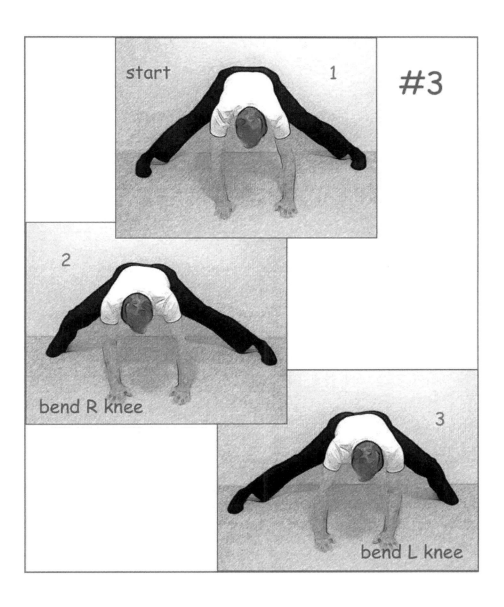

#4: Straight Leg Stretch, One Side

BENEFITS: This stretch has the same beneficial effect as #5, but focuses on one leg at a time. If you are coming off an injury, or if one leg is more prone to tightness than the other, this is a good exercise to focus on whichever leg is most appropriate. Stretches hamstrings, glutes, calves, Achilles, plantar fascia, some of the inside of the leg; relieves stress on lower back. Helps avoid cramps, muscle pulls and tightness while paddling and surfing.

COMBINE WITH: A good warmup for Hip Lift exercises (#18, #19). An easier substitute for #5 (Straight Leg Stretch, Front).

HOW TO DO IT:
- Start by sitting on the floor, legs spread, and leaning forward slightly (Position 1).
- Reach over and out with one hand and touch the toes of one foot. Try to reach over the toes to the ball of the foot (Position 2).
- Turn your torso and place the other hand on your knee (Position 3). OPTIONAL: Touch your bent elbow (left elbow in the picture) to the floor.
- Finally, extend this hand to reach your foot (Position 4). Try to pull the foot back toward you, stretching the foot and ankle.

TIPS: Don't force it. If you can't do Position 3, stop at Position 2; if you can't do Position 4, stop at Position 3. You may find that one side is easier for you than the other.

This is a great exercise to do on your surfboard, either after paddling out or while waiting for a set. Let one leg hang down in the water, put the other leg up on the board, and grab your toes. After a long paddle, this will loosen your legs and your back. During long waits in the lineup, it will help avoid tightening and cramping.

#5: Straight Leg Stretch, Front

BENEFITS: This stretch is a more challenging version of #4. Stretches hamstrings, glutes, inside of the leg; relieves stress on lower back. Helps avoid cramps, spasms, muscle pulls and tightness while paddling and surfing.

COMBINE WITH: A good warmup for Hip Lift exercises (#18, #19). To focus more on stretching hamstrings, try #2 (Leg Stretch, Reach with Both Hands).

HOW TO DO IT:
- Start by sitting on the floor, legs spread, and leaning forward slightly (Position 1). Continue by reaching forward (Position 2); then reach out to your toes (Position 3). If possible, hold your toes and stretch them back toward your body.
- Move slowly! Don't bounce or shove. Let your body weight and gravity gently curve your torso from the waist.
- In Positions 1, 2, and 3, try alternately relaxing and gently arching your lower back. Feel the difference in stretch.
- In Positions 1 and 2, use your leg muscles to turn your toes up and twist your feet toward the rear (behind you). Maintain your feet this position for a few seconds, then relax. Repeat. This is a very small motion; an inch or two at most. You'll feel the difference as different parts of the inner leg are stretched.

TIPS: Don't force it. If you can't do Position 3, stop at Position 2.

Many people are prone to cramps and strains in the back of the leg or foot, especially in cold water. Since these can ruin your surf session in a hurry, it's a good idea to keep the back of your legs stretched.

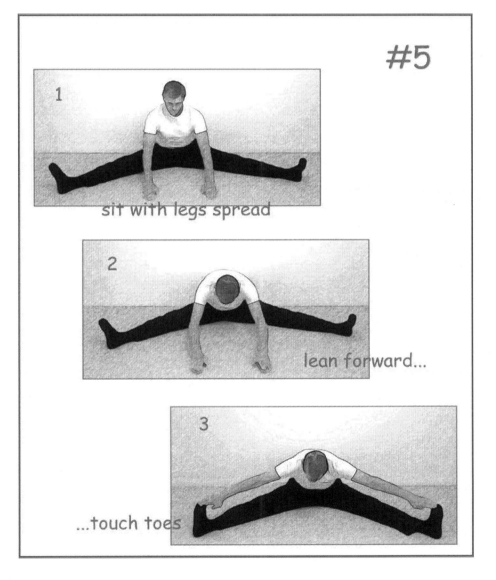

#5

1 sit with legs spread

2 lean forward...

3 ...touch toes

#6: Shoulder Stretch

BENEFITS: Maintains flexibility and range of motion in shoulder, reduces stiffness. Stretches major area used in paddling, popping up, and proning out.

COMBINE WITH: Use after any exercise making significant use of the shoulder muscles, including Four-point Stretch (#3), Agility exercises (#8 - #17), Knee Thrusts (#24 - #25) , Lateral Control (#31), all Paddling exercises (#33 - #35), and the Gull (#36).

HOW TO DO IT:
- Stand facing a wall, smooth door, or door frame.
- Place feet about one foot from the flat surface that you're facing.
- Reach one hand up and onto your back, palm resting between your shoulders. Leave the other arm down and relaxed.
- Rise up on your toes and lean into the wall or doorway, so that your bent upper arm is against the flat surface. Let your hips move forward against the wall. This will slightly arch your back.
- Lower your weight to a normal stance, still leaning your upper arm against the door or wall. Keep your hips close to the door or wall. This movement will create a stretching as your shoulder joint is opened by the gentle pressure. Hold for a few seconds on each side (1a, 1b).

Vary the stretch by changing your angle to the wall (2a, 2b).

TIPS: As with any stretch, don't force it, and stay relaxed.

The shoulders do a lot of work when surfing, and they can cause problems if not treated properly.   Stretching is an excellent preservative!

facing wall   #6

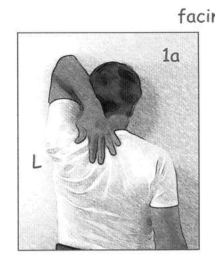
1a
L

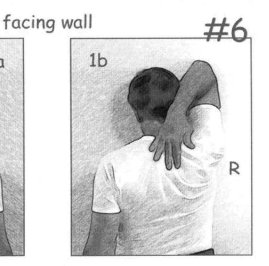
1b
R

slight angle to wall

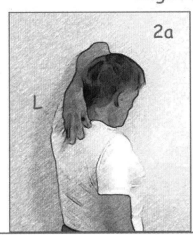
2a
L

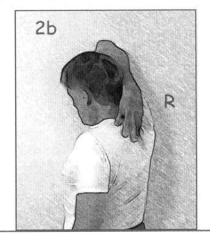
2b
R

#7: Neck Stretches

BENEFITS: Stretches neck and head area, and connections reaching down the back. Helps keep major neck muscles and tendons flexible and elastic, stretches areas that affect the ulnar nerve; helps avoid headache caused by tight muscles in neck and head. Helps avoid cramping and stiffness of the neck; increases range of motion.

COMBINE WITH: Use after Paddling (#33 - #35) and Gull (#36).

HOW TO DO IT:
- Put your head in the desired position; stretch neck with hand pressure.
- Don't pull with your arm muscles; let the weight of your arm provide the pull. (Exception: Position 5, twist.) Keep arms as relaxed as possible.
- Keep both shoulders down and relaxed.
- Let the free arm hang loose and relaxed at your side. Do NOT use it to get leverage by grabbing the chair or bench you're sitting on; this defeats the purpose of the exercise.

Start and finish with the Front stretch (Positions 1 and 6), to maintain bilateral symmetry.

Don't force any stretching exercise. Use slow, gentle pressure.

TIPS: A great exercise to do while waiting for anything, such as your computer or gridlocked traffic. Position 5 (twist) is good when lying down or in a recliner. A good neck stretch is a great relaxer; these are good at the end of any workout and at the end of the day. A great way to relax right before going to bed.

NOTE: Do NOT do neck stretches while on your surfboard or immediately before going surfing; if you attempt to paddle or react quickly to a wave during or immediately after doing neck stretches, you risk abrupt tightening and cramping.

Section 2: Agility

Agility: both on and off the wave

#8 Foot Switch

BENEFITS: Improve and maintain agility and mobility for better footwork while surfing, while giving a brisk little workout to arms, shoulders, chest and core. A valuable part of any basic daily routine. Easier than #9 (Cross-over). A good 30-second Quickie workout.

COMBINE WITH: A good follow-up to #3 (Four-point Stretch), and a nice way to ease into #9 (Cross-over). Use as a warm-up for #12 (Cross-step with Half Pop-up). Follow with #6 (Shoulder Stretch).

HOW TO DO IT:
- Place both hands on floor, spaced a little wider than your shoulders. Place one foot in front of the other (in the illustration, the Left foot is forward; Position 1)
- Shifting all your weight onto your arms, unweight your feet and quickly switch them, so that the front foot goes to the rear as the other foot comes forward (Position 2).
- Land with the other foot forward (Position 3).
- Repeat unweighting and foot switch (Position 4).
- Land with original foot forward (Left foot in illustration).
- Repeat for 10-20 cycles (L forward + R forward = one cycle)

This is NOT a lateral scissor motion. Start and finish each motion with one foot directly in front of the other.

TIPS: Do NOT try to raise your head to look forward; it puts too much strain on your cervical spine. Look down and slightly forward, at a spot a few inches in front of your hands. Do not watch your feet; learn to know where they are by somatic feedback (feel).

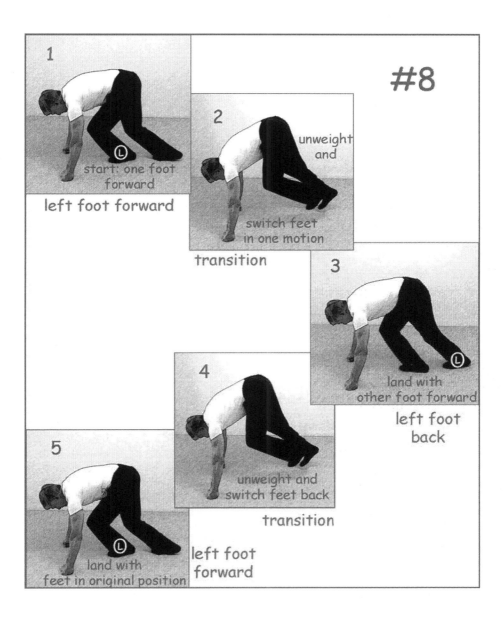

#8

1 — start: one foot forward

left foot forward

2 — unweight and switch feet in one motion

transition

3 — land with other foot forward

left foot back

4 — unweight and switch feet back

transition

left foot forward

5 — land with feet in original position

#9: Cross-Over

BENEFITS: Increase agility and mobility while working arms, shoulders, chest, back, neck, core and inner leg muscles. Improve balance and foot coordination. Improve surfing stability. More vigorous than #8 (Foot Switch). A good 30-second Quickie workout.

COMBINE WITH: Warm up with #3 (Four-point Stretch); follow with #12 (Cross-Step with Half Pop-up). Finish with #6 (Shoulder Stretch).

HOW TO DO IT:
- Put your feet about 1½ shoulder widths apart, and lean down to rest your hands on the floor (Position 1).
- Unweight your feet by shifting your weight onto your arms and lifting your knees; cross left leg in front of right leg in a scissor motion. (Position 2).
- Land with left leg crossed in front of right leg (Position 3).
- Unweight your feet again and uncross your legs (Position 4).
- Land with your feet parallel (Position 5).
- Unweight again, crossing your legs as you do so (Position 6).
- Land with legs crossed, this time right leg in front of left leg. (Position 7).
- Repeat for 10-20 cycles (cross L + cross R = one cycle).

The pattern is simple: unweight, cross - unweight, open - unweight, cross - unweight, open, etc.

The legs move in a lateral scissors motion.

TIPS: Don't watch your feet; instead look at a point slightly forward of your hands. Do NOT turn your face up to look forward; this will put strain on your cervical spine.

#9

1 start - feet parallel

2 unweight

3 L cross in front

4 unweight

5 feet parallel

6 unweight

7 R cross in front

#10: Knee Drop

BENEFITS: Strengthen arms, shoulders, chest, core, lats. Improve coordination and agility. Develop muscle connections for quick pop-ups and prone-outs when surfing. A good 30-second Quickie workout.

COMBINE WITH: A good warmup for #13 (Prone-out from Knees) and #14 (Prone-out). Finish with #6 (Shoulder Stretch).

HOW TO DO IT:
- Start in a crouching position (Position 1).
- Flex your knees and crouch down further until your hands rest on the floor (Position 2).
- Unweight your feet, shifting all your weight onto your arms (Position 3).
- Keeping your knees under your body, drop to a kneeling position (Position 4).
- To get back up to your feet, try using #11 (Pop-up from Knees).
- Repeat 5-10 times.

TIPS: Place hands on the floor fairly close together. Keep arms slightly bent for a smoother, easier motion. Don't let yourself tip too far forward.

start

#10

1

hands touch floor

2

3

feet
unweight
knees
drop

4

finish

#11: Pop-up from Knees

BENEFITS: Strengthen and condition arms, shoulder area, back, lats and body core. Build muscle connections and muscle memory for popping up. Useful if you've started riding a wave on your knees due to being caught by the breaking wave during takeoff, or stayed on your knees to take a couple of extra strokes. A good 30-second Quickie workout; warmup is advised.

COMBINE WITH: Warm up with #3 (Four-point Stretch), #8 (Foot Switch) or #9 (Cross-over). Use as a warmup for #16 (Full Pop-up) or #17 (Twisting Pop-up). Follow with #6 (Shoulder Stretch).

HOW TO DO IT:
- Kneel with hands on floor, a little wider than your shoulders (Position 1).
- Unweight your feet by shifting your weight onto your arms and driving the knees up and forward (Position 2). Feel your arms pushing down and back.
- Land with feet between your hands, either parallel (Position 3a) or with one foot advanced (Position 3b).
- To return to your knees, use #10 (Knee Drop).
- Repeat 5-10 times.

TIPS: Exhale during the motion. Keep hands and elbows close together, so that you acquire the habit of keeping your knees close together while popping up. Starting with the elbows slightly flexed creates a spring effect that makes the motion easier to execute. The main muscles used are those around and below the shoulder. Push down and back. Visualize placing the board under your feet, rather than jumping up on the board.

start on knees

#11

1

2

transition: unweight feet

3 (a)

feet parallel

3 (b)

one foot forward

#12: Cross-step (with Pop-up)

BENEFITS: Increases agility while strengthening legs, arms, shoulders, lats, abductors, abs, core.   Develops muscle memory for cross-stepping. Simulates surfing action in limited space. This is a good 30-second Quickie workout; warmup is advised.

COMBINE WITH: Warm up with #3 (Four-point Stretch), #8 (Foot Switch), #9 (Cross-over) or #23 (Knee Lift).

HOW TO DO IT:
- Start from knees, as in #11 (Position 1).
- Pop up low with one foot back (Position 2). The illustration is right foot back; if you're a goofy-foot do it your way.
- Cross-step one step with the back foot (Position 3).
- Cross-step one more step. Have fun—hang five! (Position 4).
- Cross-step back one step (Position 5).
- Cross-step back again and finish low (Position 6).
- Drop back to knees using #10 (Knee Drop).
- Repeat 5-10 times.

TIPS: Stay low—the lower, the better. The idea is to operate from a crouch. Keep hands down and forward for optimal center of gravity.
Keep your feet close and your knees tucked and tight. Get yourself used to working in a small space and moving with a low center of gravity.
Don't watch your feet—look down and to the front, being aware of the front of the board and the wave. (In the illustration, the "board" is a carpet runner 6' x 22".)

#13: Prone-Out From Knees

BENEFITS: Strengthen arms, shoulders, chest, upper body. Develop coordination and muscle memory for pop-ups, prone-outs, and whitewater situations. A good 30-second Quickie workout, but be warmed up first.

COMBINE WITH: Warm up with #3 (Four-point Stretch) or #9 (Cross-over). Try starting with #10 (Knee Drop) to create a two-stage prone-out.

HOW TO DO IT:
- Kneel on floor, both hands on floor (Position 1). You can get to your knees using #10 (Knee Drop).
- Unweight legs by shifting weight to arms and bringing knees up (Position 2). Don't drive knees forward.
- Thrust legs out and back (Position 3).
- Land prone, hands still on floor, back slightly arched (Position 4).
- To get up from this position, you can use #15, Pop-up to Knees. Or you can roll over on your back and use #17, Twisting Pop-up.
- Repeat 3-5 times.

TIPS: Don't look down between your hands; look at a point slightly in front of your hands. Keep your elbows slightly bent until the finish.
To help yourself pop back up using #15 (Pop-up to Knees) don't stop or release the muscle tension when you reach the finish (Position 4) of #13. Instead, rebound from the finish, so that when your legs and feet hit the floor, soles up (as shown in Position 4), they act like a spring to catapult you back up again.

#13

1 start

2 unweight legs

3 thrust feet back

4 finish

#14: Prone-Out

BENEFITS: Strengthens arms, shoulders, chest, upper body. Develops coordination, quickness and muscle memory for smooth, rapid transition from standing to prone position. Also develops muscles and muscle connections for better surfing. A good 30-second Good for a 30-second Quickie workout, but be warmed up first.

COMBINE WITH: Warm up with #8 (Foot Switch), #10 (Knee Drop) or #13 (Prone-out from Knees).

HOW TO DO IT:
- Start from a crouch (Position 1).
- Crouch down lower and rest your hands on the floor (Position 2).
- Shift your weight onto your arms, unweight your feet, and thrust feet and legs back (Position 3).
- Keep arms flexed and firm, so that your legs and lower torso go down first (Position 4).
- From here you can pop back up using #16 (Full Pop-up). You also can do a two-stage pop-up using #15 (Pop-up to Knees) plus #11 (Pop-up from Knees). Or you can roll over on your back and do #17 (Twisting Pop-up).
- Repeat 3-5 times

TIPS: Keep arms slightly bent until the finish. Don't lean too far forward.
To help yourself pop back up (using either #16, Full Pop-up or #15, Pop-up to Knees) don't stop or release the muscle tension when you reach the finish (Position 4) of #14. Instead, rebound from the finish, so that when your legs and feet hit the floor, soles up (as shown in Position 4), they act like a spring to catapult you back up again.

1 start

#14

2 hands touch floor

3 feet unweight & thrust back

4 finish

#15: Pop-Up To Knees

BENEFITS: Works shoulders, arms, back, lats, core, abductors, abs. Develops coordination, quickness and muscle memory needed for pop-up. A good 30-second Quickie workout, but be warmed up first.

COMBINE WITH: Warm up with #3 (Four-point Stretch), #23 (Knee Lift), #24 (Single Knee Thrust), or #25 (Alternating Knee Thrust). Use as a warmup for #16 (Full Pop-up).

HOW TO DO IT:
- Lie on floor, back arched, hands on floor, hands near lower ribs (Position 1).
- Use back arch and arm push to lift upper torso from floor (Position 2).
- Use arch, arm push and foot thrust to unweight legs; drive knees forward (Position 3).
- Drive knees low, between shoulders (Position 4).
- Finish in kneeling position (Position 5).
- To return to the prone position, you can do #13 (Prone-out from Knees).
- Repeat 3-5 times.

TIPS: Use a quick push of your feet against the board as a spring to catapult your legs and hips up and forward. Exhale through the motion. Keep arms flexed throughout. Keep hands fairly close together, to ensure that your legs remain close together as you drive your knees between your elbows.

Useful if you're 90% into a wave that backs off or refuses to jack up; you can pop up to your knees, take a few strokes, and then stand up when the wave gets steeper.

#15

1 start

2 arch back

3 unweight feet...
   drive knees forward

4 knees under shoulders

5 finish

#16: Full Pop-Up

BENEFITS: Works shoulders, arms, back, lats, core, abductors, abs. Develops coordination, quickness and muscle memory needed for pop-up. A good 30-second Quickie workout, but be warmed up first.

COMBINE WITH: Warm up with #3 (Four-point Stretch), #23 (Knee Lift), #24 (Single Knee Thrust), or #25 (Alternating Knee Thrust). You can also start with #11 (Pop-up from Knees).

HOW TO DO IT:
- Lie on floor, back arched, hands on floor, hands near lower ribs (Position 1).
- Use arch, arm push and foot thrust to unweight legs; drive knees forward (Position 2).
- Drive knees low, between shoulders (Position 3).
- Bring feet under body (Position 4).
- Finish in surfing position, one foot forward (Position 5).
- To return to the prone position, use #14 (Prone-out).
- Repeat 3-5 times.

TIPS: Starting with the back arched creates a better angle and generates a spring effect that makes the motion easier to execute. Use a quick push of your feet against the floor as a spring to catapult your legs and hips up and forward. Exhale through the motion. Keep arms flexed throughout. Keep hands fairly close together, to ensure that your legs remain close together as you drive your knees between your elbows.

#16

1 arch back

2 unweight feet

3 knees come forward

4 pop up low

5 finish

#17: Twisting Pop-Up

BENEFITS: Studies have shown that the best single exercise, the one that works the most muscle groups with zero impact, is the simple act of lying down on the floor and getting up again. Here's a variation that develops body core, abductors, abs, shoulders, arms; agility, timing.   Develops spatial orientation.   Good 30-second Quickie workout if warmed up first.

COMBINE WITH: Warm up with #8 (Foot Switch), #9 (Cross-over) or #11 (Pop-up from Knees). Use to get up after any floor exercise.

HOW TO DO IT:
- Quickly! The idea is not to clamber up, but to pop up while twisting.
- Sit up and twist at the same time. Quickly. Notice that only the hips are touching the ground (Position 2). Knees start toward body.
- Cross over in a continuous turning motion and bring hands to floor (Position 3). Knees bend further, top foot goes to floor.
- Put weight on hands and unweight feet, bringing knees forward (Position 4).
- Finish the motion (Positions 5 and 6).
- Do the exercise both to the left and to the right, repeating each side 3-5 times.

You can either switch sides each time, or do one side a few times to get the motion down, then do the same number of repetitions on the other side.

TIPS: If you're turning to the **right** (as in the illustration), cross your **left** hand and foot over and around. (Position 3). To twist up to the **left**, cross your **right** hand and foot over and around.

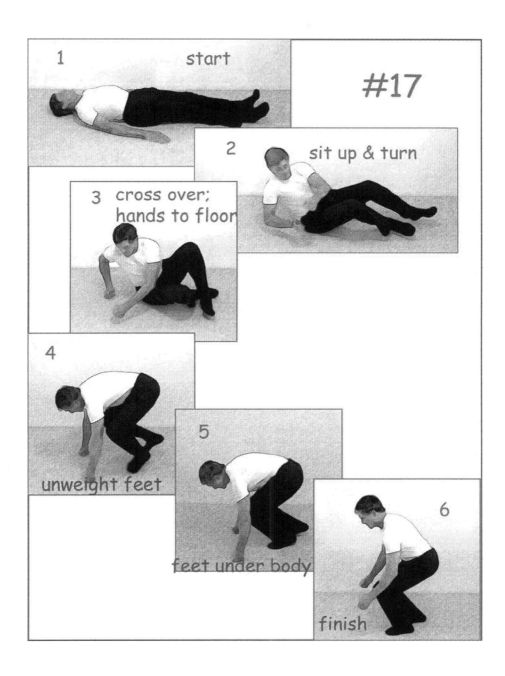

1 start

#17

2 sit up & turn

3 cross over;
hands to floor

4

unweight feet

5

feet under body

6

finish

Section 3: Legs, Hips, Core, Lower body

Surfing requires 3-D leg strength

Float through the foam

On a late takeoff or unmakeable section, use weight shift and foot and leg control to keep your board horizontal as you float across and down through the breaking wave.

If you do a few of the agility exercises in Section 2, you'll find that many of them are excellent for developing leg strength. For example, if you repeat Pop-up from Knees (#11) or Cross-step with Pop-up (#12) a half-dozen times, you will definitely feel the benefits in your quads and other leg muscles.

The exercises in Section 3 focus more closely on working all parts of the legs and hip area, including the glutes. They also develop, condition and strengthen the core and lower body.

It's important to work all sides of the hip and leg area—front, back, inside and outside. Although the hamstrings and quads are perhaps the key areas, in turbulent conditions such as violent whitewash, or when making a recovery or a sudden move (as when a foot slips off the rail), hitting a patch of kelp or other unexpected event, many other muscle groups come into play. The strength, elasticity and flexibility of these muscles and related connective tissue can be the difference between making the wave and getting thrashed, or between finishing a session and leaving the water early with a muscle pull or torn ligament.

#18: Hip Lift

#18A is done with the knees bent at about a 90 degree angle; when pushing against the floor to raise the hips, the lower leg is almost vertical. This works the lower back more.

#18B is done with the legs partially extended. This works the hamstrings and back of the leg more, and provides more exercise for the ankle and foot.

BENEFITS: Tones and strengthens body core, glutes, rear of leg, hip area, back, neck. Strengthens muscle groups essential for paddling. Good for recovery from "banana peel" type falls.

COMBINE WITH: Warm up with Four-point Stretch (#3). Alternate with the Turtle (#22). Follow with any Straight Leg Stretch (#1, #2, #5, #6).

HOW TO DO IT:

- Lie on your back, face up. Both feet on floor, knees bent about 90 degrees (Position 1).
- Push feet against floor to raise hips (Position 2). Pause briefly, then lower and repeat.
- Repeat 10-50 times, at a rate of about 1 per second.
- Do the same with your legs extended further from the hips, as in version B (Positions 3 and 4). Feel the difference.

You can leave your head resting on the floor, or keep it slightly raised. Do NOT do neck curls (raising and lowering your head) ; they're hard on your cervical spine.

TIPS: Try moving your feet to various distances from your hips, to work different sets of muscles. Don't rush, just keep a nice, smooth flow. Do NOT bridge with your neck, shoulders or arms. Keep your weight on your feet and on your upper back.

1
hips down

#18 (A)

hip lift normal

2
hips up

#18 (B)

3
hips down

hip lift extended

hips up

4

#19: Hip Lift, One Leg

Shown with #18 for comparison. The motion is the same, but in #19 one leg is kept raised throughout, so that only one leg is doing the work of raising and lowering the hips.

BENEFITS: Tones and strengthens body core, glutes, rear of leg, hip area, back, neck. Strengthens muscle groups essential for paddling. Good for recovery from "banana peel" type falls.

COMBINE WITH: Warm up with Four-point Stretch (#3). Alternate with the Turtle (#22). Follow with any Straight Leg Stretch (#1, #2, #5, #6).

HOW TO DO IT:
- Lie on your back, face up. Both feet on floor, knees bent about 90 degrees. Raise and lower hips a few times (Positions 1 and 2).
- With hips down, raise one leg and hold it there (Position 3).
- Raise hips by pushing the other foot against the floor (Position 4). Pause briefly, then lower hips and repeat, keeping one leg up.
- Repeat 5-20 times, at a rate of about 1 per second.
- Change feet and repeat.
- Always start and finish with a few (5-10) repetitions of Positions 1 and 2 (#18), to maintain bilateral symmetry and avoid strain.

Leave your head resting on the floor, or keep it slightly raised. Do NOT do neck curls (raising and lowering your head); they're hard on your cervical spine.

TIPS: Try moving your supporting foot to various distances from your hips, to work different sets of muscles. Don't rush, just keep a nice, smooth flow. Do NOT bridge with your neck, shoulders or arms. Keep your weight on your foot and on your upper back.

1
hips down
both feet on floor

#18

2
hips up

3
hips down
keep one leg raised

#19

4
hips up

#20: Straight Leg Raises, Side

BENEFITS: Works hip, leg, side, neck; flexibility, general conditioning. Works muscle groups used to get back up on your board when you're in the water. Great for bodyboarding and bodysurfing.

COMBINE WITH: Scissor (#21) to work inside of leg; Hip Lift (#18, #19) for a complete leg workout. Alternate with Turtle (#22). Follow with any Straight Leg Stretch (#1, #2, #5, #6).

HOW TO DO IT (A):
- Lie on one side, looking straight ahead (Position 1).
- Keeping head and body still, raise top leg (Position 2) and lower it again (Position 1).
- Repeat 5-20 times.

HOW TO DO IT (B):
- Lie on one side and turn head to face up (Position 3).
- Keeping head and body still, raise top leg (Position 4) and lower it again (Position 3).
- Repeat 5-20 times.

HOW TO DO IT (A+B):
- Do A, then B, then A.
- Start and finish with A to maintain bilateral symmetry.

TIPS: Don't rush. Use a smooth, steady motion to raise the leg. Don't bend your neck, keep the cervical vertebrae in line.

Do NOT rest your head on the floor; doing so will put your neck at an angle.

#20 (A)

1 leg down

leg up

looking straight

2

#20 (B)

3 leg down

head turned looking up

leg up

4

#21: Scissor

BENEFITS: Strengthens inside of leg, groin, neck, side, body core; develops coordination of muscle groups. Develops strength and muscle sequence used in a variety of surfing and bodysurfing situations.

COMBINE WITH: Straight Leg Raises, Side (#20); Turtle (#22); Hip Lift (#18, #19). Follow with Four-point Stretch (#3) or Straight Leg Stretch (#4, #5).

HOW TO DO IT (A):
- Lie on one side, looking straight ahead, with left leg crossed over right leg, sole of left foot on floor (Position 1).
- Keeping head and body still, raise right leg in a scissor motion (Position 2) and lower it again (Position 1).
- Repeat 20-50 times.

HOW TO DO IT (B):
- Lie on one side as in (A), with head turned to face up (Position 3).
- Keeping head and body still, raise right leg in a scissor motion (Position 4) and lower it again (Position 3).
- Repeat 20-50 times.

HOW TO DO IT (A+B):
- Do A, then B, then A.
- Start and finish with A to maintain bilateral symmetry.

TIPS: Do not rest your head on the floor; keep cervical spine straight. Don't jerk, but use a single strong motion. This motion is quicker than the leg raising motion in Straight Leg Raises, Side (#20).

Do NOT rest your head on the floor; doing so will put your neck at an angle.

#21 (A)

1 start: L leg over R

looking straight

2 scissor raising R leg

#21 (B)

3 start: L leg over R

head turned looking up

4 scissor raising R leg

#22: The Turtle

BENEFITS: Strengthens body core, abductors, abs, lower back, neck. There is a lot more to this than meets the eye. A good 30-second Quickie exercise.

COMBINE WITH: Alternate with Hip Lifts (#18, #19), Straight Leg Stretches (#1, #2, #4, #5).

HOW TO DO IT:
- Lie on floor, back flat on floor, knees and feet up as shown.
- Keep head raised slightly off of floor; arms around legs but NOT touching or pushing legs.
- Compress by using leg muscles to squeeze knees together while using abductors to squeeze knees toward chest. Do NOT use arms or hands to press on legs.
- At the same time, press lower back against floor to straighten lower spine.
- Exhale on the squeeze.
- Release pressure while inhaling.
- Repeat 3-10 times.

Do NOT use your arms or hands to push or squeeze. Keep your arms and hands relaxed; their position is merely for better balance and body dynamics.

You may rest head on floor, or keep it slightly elevated to involve the neck muscles. Do NOT raise and lower your head as you do the exercise.

#22

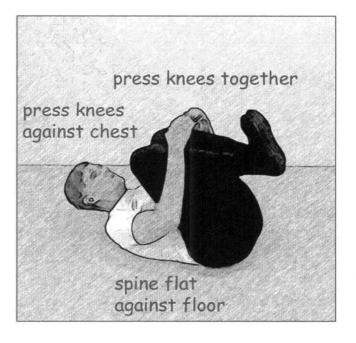

#23: Knee Lift

BENEFITS: Strengthens abductors, abs, body core. Very good for overall conditioning. Good preparation for surfing pop-ups. A good exercise for improving balance. Good 30-second Quickie workout.

COMBINE WITH: Warm up with Four-point Stretch (#3) or Foot Switch (#8). Follow with Pop-up from Knees (#11).

HOW TO DO IT:
- Stand erect, feet about one shoulder width apart, palms down in front of chin; arms parallel to floor.
- Legs straight but not stiff or locked.
- Raise one knee to palm of hand.
- Lower knee.
- Repeat 5-20 times with each leg.

It's best to do several reps with one leg, then change legs.

TIPS: Do NOT throw or jerk your knee upward. The motion should be quick but smooth. Use a strong, steady drive to thrust the knee upward.

Feel free to rest your hips against a counter-top, or have a wall behind your back for balance. Do NOT lean backward.

If you choose to do the knee lift without support, be sure to keep your spine straight and body erect.

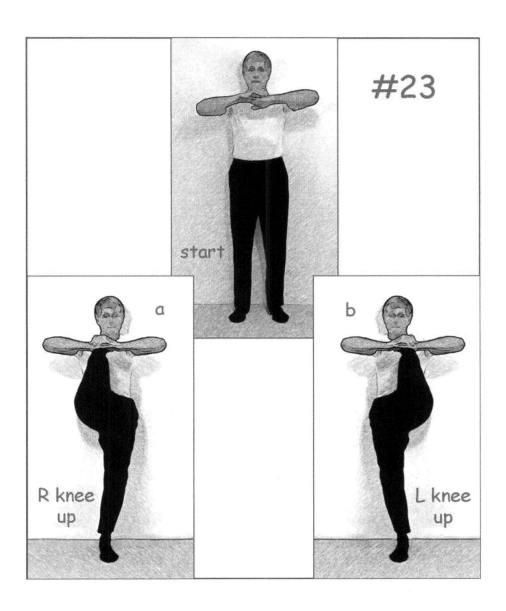

#23

start

a

b

R knee
up

L knee
up

#24: Single Knee Thrust

BENEFITS: Strengthens shoulders, arms, back, abductors, abs. Develops muscle connections and muscle memory essential to popping up quickly. A good 30-second Quickie workout.

COMBINE WITH: Warm up with Four-point Stretch (#3) or Foot Switch (#8). Follow up with Shoulder Stretch (#6). A good complement to Cross-over (#9). A good warmup for Alternating Knee Thrust (#25).

HOW TO DO IT.
- Put your feet about a shoulder width apart, and lean down to rest your hands on the floor (Position 1).
- Keeping your weight on both hands and your right foot, drive your left knee toward a spot between your elbows. (Positions 2, 3).
- Immediately bring the knee back (Position 4) to the starting point (Position 5).
- Either repeat several times with same knee, or alternate knees each time.
- Repeat until you've done each knee 10-20 times.

TIPS: Do NOT look at your feet. Look at a point slightly in front of your hands. Imagine it's the front portion of a surfboard. Do NOT tip your head back to look far forward; it puts stress on your cervical spine.

#24

1
start:
feet parallel

2
transition

3
L foot forward

4
transition

5
back to start

#25: Alternating Knee Thrust

BENEFITS: Strengthens shoulders, arms, abductors, abs, body core; develops agility and coordination. Builds muscle memory and musculature required for quick pop-ups. Good conditioning for short-term bursts of output. A good 30-second Quickie workout.

COMBINE WITH: Warm up with Four-point Stretch (#3) or Foot Switch (#8). A good complement to Cross-over (#9). Use as warmup for Pop-up from Knees (#11). Follow up with Shoulder Stretch (#6).

HOW TO DO IT:
- Lean over, rest both hands on the floor, and advance left foot as far as possible, keeping your right leg straight but not locked. This is your starting position. (Position 1).
- Unweight your feet by shifting weight onto your arms and lifting your knees. Your hips may rise as a result. At the same time, switch feet, driving your right knee forward and your left foot back. (Position 2).
- Land in a mirror image of your starting position, with your right foot now in front and left leg straight but not locked (Position 3).
- Repeat the switch and reverse feet again (Position 4).
- Land in your original position, left foot forward. (Position 5),
- Repeat for 10-20 cycles. (L forward + R forward = 1 cycle.)

TIPS: Do NOT look at your feet. Look at a point slightly in front of your hands. Imagine it's the front portion of a surfboard. Do NOT tip your head back to look far forward; it puts stress on your cervical spine.

#25

1 left foot forward

2 switch

3 right foot forward

4 switch

5 left foot forward

Section 4: Arms, Shoulders, Back, Upper body

Arm, shoulder and upper-body strength is essential

As you've seen, Sections 1 through 3 include exercises where the arms, shoulders and upper body are in a secondary role, but get significant benefits. Examples include #3 (Four-point Stretch), #8 (Foot Switch), #9 (Cross-over), #10-#17 (all the various drops, prone-outs and pop-ups), and #24-#25 (Knee Thrusts).

The exercises in Section 4 are designed to target the muscle groups and develop the stamina needed for paddling and board control. For this reason, they are aimed at endurance and conditioning more than pure strength.

When doing the exercises with weights, don't rush, and don't throw or jerk the weights. Maintain push or thrust all the way through the motion. Move with a smooth, brisk pace (about 2-3 strokes per second, depending on the exercise) and rhythmic, even breathing. You might do anywhere from 50 to 200 repetitions, again depending on the exercise. When doing the Gull (#36), 50 reps is plenty; when doing Paddling, Crawl Style (#33) you might do 100 strokes or so; Curls (#26) might go as high as 200 or more.

Remember, these numbers are not minimums or requirements, or even goals. Do what you feel you need and what you feel like doing. You'll find that over time, your body will find its own best level of intensity and duration. Before long you will have developed your own pace and your own set of numbers for each workout. Once you do, you'll find it remarkably easy to maintain.

#26: Curls

BENEFITS: Develop and condition biceps, wrists, shoulders, neck, shoulder area.   Work muscle groups involved in board control; improve neck strength and range of motion. Develop countervailing muscle groups involved in paddling.

COMBINE WITH: Reverse Curls (#29, #30), Water-glass Lift (#32), Paddling (#33, #34), Gull (#36).

HOW TO DO IT:
- Hold one weight in each hand, palms to the front.
- Full curl: extend one arm down, straight but not locked; bring other hand up by bending elbow.
- Bend the straight elbow while straightening the bent elbow.
- Half curl: same as full curl, but instead of extending arm down, lower the hand only until the forearm is horizontal.
- Head turned: do both half and full curls looking forward, and also with your head turned to the side.

TRY THIS SEQUENCE (1 left + 1 right = 1 cycle):
- Half curl 50 cycles: 10 looking front, 10 looking to the right, 10 front, 10 looking left, 10 front.
- Full curl 50 cycles: 10 front, 10 right, 10 front, 10 left, 10 front.

When your head is turned, look over your shoulder. Do NOT swivel your neck from side to side.   Start and finish looking forward to maintain bilateral symmetry.

TIPS: Start with half curls to warm up, then do full curls.
Pace: between 1 and 2 cycles (1 left + 1 right = 1 cycle) per second.

#26

looking front

full curl

head turned to side

half curl

#27: Rotator Open And Closed

BENEFITS: Toning, stretching and strengthening rotator cuff and shoulder area, and increasing range of motion. Improve board control and retention if caught inside on bigger days.

COMBINE WITH: Turtle (#22), Lateral Control (#31), Reverse Curls (#29, #30). Get up using Twisting Pop-up (#17).

HOW TO DO IT (A):
- Lie on back, knees bent 90 degrees, elbows resting on floor next to body, elbows bent 90 degrees, forearms vertical (Position 1).
- Rotate arms outward, allowing hands to move toward the floor, keeping elbows resting on floor (Position 2).
- Rotate the other direction to bring forearms back to vertical and return to Position 1.
- Repeat 5-15 times.

HOW TO DO IT (B):
- Lie on back with left arm rotated outward as in A1, and with your right arm resting across your chest (Position 3).
- Rotate both arms in the same direction, like a windshield wiper, keeping elbows close to body (Position 4).
- Rotate back down to Position 3.
- Repeat 5-15 times.
- Start and finish with (A) to maintain bilateral symmetry.

Pace: about 1 cycle (1 cycle = open/close or up/back) per second.

TIPS: Do NOT jerk or rush. Use a steady, strong motion. Do NOT force your hands down; bring them down naturally. Keep elbows close to body and bent 90 degrees. Let your head rest on the floor. Use less weight if that is more comfortable for you.

#28: Rotator Plus Hip Lift

BENEFITS: Increases strength, flexibility and range of motion in shoulders; works legs, glutes, back, body core.

COMBINE WITH: Warm up with Rotator Open and Closed (#27). Finish with Four-Point Stretch (#3) or Straight Leg Stretch (#1, #2, #4). Get up using Twisting Pop-up (#17). Goes well with Turtle (#22), Lateral Control (#31), Reverse Curls (#29, #30).

HOW TO DO IT (A):
- Lie on back, knees bent 90 degrees, elbows resting on floor next to body, elbows bent 90 degrees, forearms vertical (Position 1).
- Rotate arms outward, allowing hands to move toward the floor, keeping elbows resting on floor close to body (Position 2).
- Rotate the other direction to bring forearms back to vertical and return to Position 1.
- Repeat 5-15 times. Pace: about 1 cycle (1 cycle = open/close or up/back) per second.

HOW TO DO IT (B):
- Lie on back with left arm rotated outward as in A1, and with your right arm resting across your chest (Position 3).
- Rotate both arms in the same direction, like a windshield wiper, keeping elbows close to body (Position 4).
- Rotate back down to Position 3.
- Repeat 5-15 times. Pace: about 1 cycle (1 cycle = open/close or up/back) per second.
- Start and finish with (A) to maintain bilateral symmetry.

TIPS: Do NOT jerk or rush. Use a steady, strong motion. Do NOT force your hands down; bring them down naturally. Keep elbows close to body and bent 90 degrees. Let your head rest on the floor. Use less weight if that is more comfortable for you.

start

#28 (A)

keep elbows bent
90 degrees

rotate open & down

lift hips

1

2

#28 (B)

start   3

keep one leg up

rotate open & down

keep elbows bent
90 degrees

4

lift hips

#29: Reverse Curls; With Hip Lift

BENEFITS: Develop coordination and timing; strengthen and condition arms, hips, legs, lower back, shoulders, body core. Works major muscle groups used in paddling.

COMBINE WITH: Warm up and finish with Four-point Stretch (#3) or Straight Leg Stretch (#1, #2, #4, #5). Get up using Twisting Pop-up (#17). Goes well with Turtle (#22), Lateral Control (#31).

HOW TO DO IT (A):
- Lie on your back, feet flat, knees bent about 90 degrees. Hold one weight in each hand. One arm bent, the other extended toward the ceiling (Position 1).
- Extend bent arm while bending the extended arm (Position 2).
- Repeat 5-50 cycles (1 left + 1 right = 1 cycle).

HOW TO DO IT (B):
- Lift your hips as the LEFT arm goes up and lower them as the RIGHT arm goes up (Positions 3 and 4).
- Repeat 5-50 cycles (1 left + 1 right = 1 cycle).
- Reverse the arms: lift the hips as the RIGHT arm goes up and lower them as the LEFT arm goes up (Positions 3 and 4 reversed).
- Repeat 5-50 cycles (1 left + 1 right = 1 cycle).

Pattern: up-down-up-down combined with L-R-L-R, then with R-L-R-L. Pace: about one cycle per second.

TIPS: Let your head rest on the floor. Vary the effect by extending the bent (down) arm slightly along the floor (to the right in the illustration).

extend R arm

1

keep hips on floor

#29 (A)

extend L arm

2

#29 (B)

3

extend R arm

hips down

raise hips &
extend L arm

4

hips up

#30: Reverse Curls With Hip Lift, One Leg

BENEFITS: Develop coordination and timing; strengthen and condition arms, hips, legs, lower back, shoulders, body core. Works major muscle groups used in paddling.

COMBINE WITH: Warm up and finish with Four-point Stretch (#3) or Straight Leg Stretch (#1, #2, #4, #5). Get up using Twisting Pop-up (#17). Goes well with Turtle (#22), Lateral Control (#31).

HOW TO DO IT (A):
- Lie on your back, feet flat, knees bent about 90 degrees. Hold one weight in each hand. One arm bent, the other extended toward the ceiling (Position 1).
- Lift your hips as the LEFT arm goes up and lower them as the RIGHT arm goes up (Position 2).
- Repeat 5-50 cycles (1 left + 1 right = 1 cycle).
- Reverse the arms: lift the hips as the RIGHT arm goes up and lower them as the LEFT arm goes up (Position 2 reversed).
- Repeat 5-50 cycles.

HOW TO DO IT (B):
- With hips down, raise one leg and keep it up.
- Lift your hips as the LEFT arm goes up and lower them as the RIGHT arm goes up (Position 2).
- Repeat 5-20 cycles (1 left + 1 right = 1 cycle).
- Reverse the arm/leg relation, leading with the other arm.
- Repeat 5-20 cycles (1 left + 1 right = 1 cycle).

Pattern: up-down-up-down combined with L-R-L-R, then with R-L-R-L. Pace: about one cycle per second.

TIPS: Let your head rest on the floor. Start and finish with (A).

hips down,
extend R arm

1

keep both feet
on floor

#30 (A)

raise hips &
extend L arm

2

hips up

hips down,
extend R arm

3

keep one leg raised

#30 (B)

raise hips &
extend L arm

4

hips up

#31: Lateral Control

BENEFITS: Strengthen chest, shoulder area, arms, glutes, core. Develop strength and muscle groups needed to control your board when popping up on a bumpy or breaking wave and when duck-diving or rolling through larger waves. A good 30-second Quickie workout.

COMBINE WITH: Warm up and finish with Four-point Stretch (#3) or Straight Leg Stretch (#1, #2, #4, #5). Get up using Twisting Pop-up (#17). Goes well with Turtle (#22), Rotator (#27, #28), Reverse Curls (#29, #30).

HOW TO DO IT:
- Lie on floor, back straight, feet at a comfortable separation, knees bent about 90 degrees. Keep head off floor.
- Start with elbows bent 90 degrees and upper arms out to the sides (Position 1).
- Bring right arm inward a few inches while moving the left arm back a few inches. This is not a large motion, less than one foot.
- Reverse the motion, bringing left arm in and right arm out.
- Repeat 20-50 cycles (1 right + 1 left = 1 cycle).

Replicate the feeling of trying to hang onto and stabilize a board as it is whiplashed from one side to the other by chop or turbulence.

Pace: about 1 cycle per second.

TIPS: Use firm, solid motions and a fairly quick tempo. With each arm shift you should feel pressure moving from one foot to the other, and muscles tensing in your core, glutes and legs as your feet push against the floor. Try moving your feet closer together to vary the muscles used.

start   1

elbows bent
90 degreees

#31

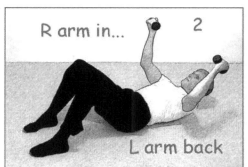

R arm in...   2

L arm back

L arm in...   3

R arm back

#32: Water-glass Lift

BENEFITS: Warms up shoulders. Develops and conditions arms, shoulders, upper body, back, neck. Stretches and tones glutes and back of legs. (Good for shoulders; derived from an exercise used by baseball pitchers.)

COMBINE WITH: Use as warmup for all Paddling (#33-#35) and for the Gull (#36). Finish with Shoulder Stretch (#6), Neck Stretch (#7).

HOW TO DO IT:
- Stand with feet parallel, about 1½ shoulder widths apart, legs straight but not stiff or locked. Arms down, palms facing each other (inward). Bend from the waist.
- Bring one arm up and back, keeping the palm facing in. Do NOT rotate wrist; at the top of the motion the axis of the mini-dumbbell should be close to vertical. (At the top of the motion, imagine that you are holding a full glass of water right-side up, and trying to keep from spilling it.)
- Bring this arm down to the starting position, while bringing the other arm up and back.
- Repeat 10-40 cycles (1 left + 1 right = 1 cycle) in each position (facing straight, looking left, looking right). Pace: about one cycle (2 strokes) per second.
- Start and finish in the original (face straight) position.

Do NOT swivel your neck back and forth; it's bad for your cervical spine. Do at least 2-5 reps in one position before turning your head.

TIPS: Don't jerk or throw your arms. Use a strong, steady motion.
Minimize upper body rotation, especially when turning head to side.
Do NOT try to tip your head back to look forward; maintain good neck posture to avoid stress to cervical spine.

#33: Paddling, Crawl Style

BENEFITS: Strengthen and condition back, glutes, legs, shoulders, lats, arms, neck. Develop stronger, faster paddling.

COMBINE WITH: Warm-up with Water-glass Lift (#32). Finish with Shoulder Stretch (#6), Neck Stretch (#7). Goes well with Paddling Two-hand (#34), Gull (#36), Canoe Paddle (#35).

HOW TO DO IT:
- Hold one weight in each hand, palms back. Lean forward. Keep knees straight but not locked. Keep shaft of weight horizontal.
- Swing one hand up and to the rear, palm up, elbow straight but not locked. Leave the other arm down (Position1). Do NOT rotate wrist; keep shaft of weight horizontal.
- As this hand comes down, the other hand goes up (Position 2).
- Repeat for 5-20 cycles (1 left + 1 right = 1 cycle).
- Now turn your head to one side and keep it there (Positions 3, 4).
- Continue the same arm motion for 5-20 cycles.
- Turn your neck to face straight again (Positions 1, 2).
- Continue the same arm motion for 5-20 cycles.
- Turn your head to the other side and keep it there (Positions 3, 4), continuing the same arm motion for 5-20 cycles.
- Face straight again (Positions 1,2) and finish up with a final 5-20 cycles.

Do NOT swivel head back and forth. Do front, one side, front, other side, front. Repeat the entire set if desired.

Pace: about one cycle (2 strokes) per second.

TIPS: Don't rush, jerk or throw the hand back, just apply a steady pressure through the stroke. Do NOT crane your neck back to look forward; it will put strain on your cervical spine. Look DOWN at a point slightly in front of your head.

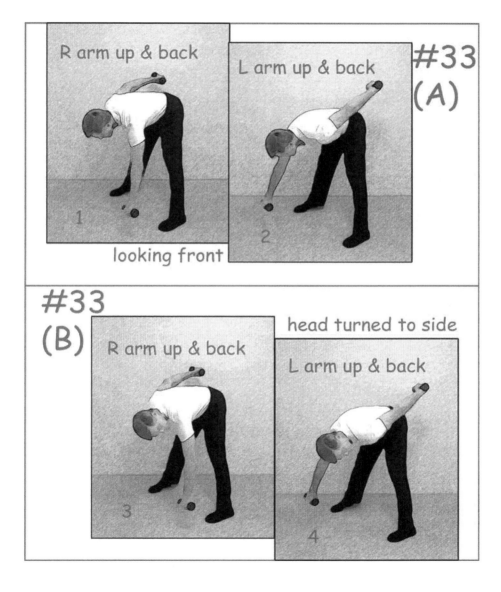

#34: Paddling, Two-Hand Style

BENEFITS: Strengthen and condition back, glutes, legs, shoulders, lats, arms, neck. Develop stronger, faster paddling.

COMBINE WITH: Warm-up with Water-glass Lift (#32). Finish with Shoulder Stretch (#6), Neck Stretch (#7). Goes well with Paddling Crawl (#33), Gull (#36), Canoe Paddle (#35).

HOW TO DO IT:
- Hold one weight in each hand, palms back. Lean forward, hands down. Knees straight, not locked. Shaft of weight horizontal (parallel to floor). (Position1)
- Swing both hands up and to the rear, palms up. Keep the elbows straight but not locked (Position2). Do NOT rotate wrist; keep shaft of weight horizontal (parallel to floor).
- Bring arms back down.
- Repeat 5-10 times. Pace: about one stroke per second.
- Turn head to one side and keep it there (Positions 3, 4).
- Continue the same arm motion 5-10 times.
- Face straight again (Positions 1, 2) and continue the same arm motion 5-10 times.
- Turn head to the other side and keep it there (Positions 3, 4).
- Continue the same arm motion 5-10 times.
- Face straight again (Positions 1,2) and finish with 5-10 strokes.

Do NOT swivel head back and forth. Do straight, one side, straight, other side, straight. Repeat the entire set if desired.

Pace: about one stroke per second.

TIPS: Don't rush, jerk or throw the hand back, just apply a steady pressure through the stroke. Do NOT crane your neck back to look forward; it will put strain on your cervical spine. Look DOWN at a point slightly in front of your head.

1

start down

looking straight

up & back

2

#34
(A)

#34
(B)

head
turned
to side

3

start down

up & back

4

#35: Canoe Paddle

BENEFITS: Develops and conditions arms, shoulders, upper body, back. Stretches and tones glutes and back of legs.

COMBINE WITH: Warm up with Water-glass Lift (#32). Use with Gull (#36). Finish with Shoulder Stretch (#6), Neck Stretch (#7).

HOW TO DO IT:
- Stand with feet parallel, about 1½ shoulder widths apart, legs straight but not stiff or locked. Arms down, palms facing each other (inward). Bend from the waist.
- Bring one arm up and back and the other arm across the body and back as if paddling with a paddle. Do not roll hands over; keep them aligned as if holding a paddle. Hand position of upper hand is similar to Water-glass Lift (#32).
- Bring arms down and repeat.
- Repeat 10-40 times on one side, then switch sides.

It's more effective to do 10-40 reps on one side rather than switching sides after each stroke or two.

TIPS: Minimize upper body rotation. Keep upper body as still as possible and use arms, shoulders and back to generate the motion. Don't turn your head to the side. Don't jerk or throw your arms. Use a firm, steady motion. Pace: about one stroke per second.

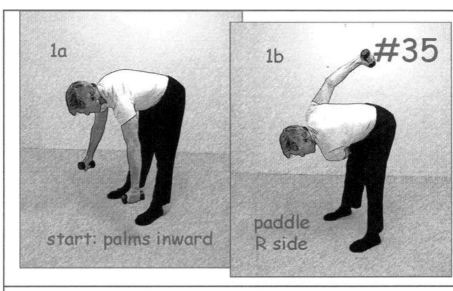

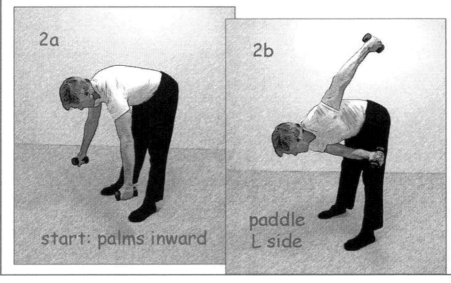

#36: The Gull

BENEFITS: Strengthen and condition back, arms, neck, legs, glutes. Build strength and endurance for recovery stroke when paddling.

COMBINE WITH: Warm up with Water-glass Lift (#32). Finish with Shoulder Stretch (#6), Neck Stretch (#7). Goes well with Paddling (#33-#35).

HOW TO DO IT:
- Hold one weight in each hand, palms back—axis of weight approximately vertical.
- Bend from the waist, knees straight but not locked, arms hanging down at your sides.
- Swing your arms up and out to the sides (not back) until they're horizontal (Position 1). Palms back; do NOT rotate wrist or arm.
- Raise arms a few inches toward the ceiling (Position 2).
- Lower to Position 1. Repeat 5-10 times.
- Turn head to one side and continue the same gentle up and down motion (Positions 3, 4).
- Repeat 5-10 times.
- Look straight, continuing the same arm movement (Positions 1, 2); repeat 5-10 times.
- Turn head to other side, continuing the same arm movement (Positions 3, 4); repeat 5-10 times.
- Look straight again, continuing arm motion (Positions 1, 2).

NO huge motions, just a few inches. Do NOT swivel your head from side to side. Do straight, turned, straight, turned, straight.
Pace: about 1 cycle (up/down) per second.

TIPS: Unlike Paddling exercises, keep shaft of weight more or less vertical; arm motion is up and down, not back. Do NOT look up to the front; this is not good for your neck.

down

up

#36 (A)

looking straight
1
2

down

head turned to side # #36 (B)

up

3
4

Get used to looking both ways for traffic

30-second Mini-workouts

All of the exercises in this program can be done with enough intensity and duration to be effective in two minutes or less. Several of them require even less time. Here are a dozen "Quickie" exercises that make excellent 30-second mini-workouts when you're pressed for time, just want a quick break from TV or the computer, or want to get the circulation going before a surf session. None of these requires any weights or other equipment. They are:

- Foot Switch (#8)
- Cross-over (#9)
- Pop-up from Knees (#11)*
- Cross-step (#12)*
- Pop-up to Knees (#15)*
- Full Pop-up (#16)*
- Twisting Pop-up (#17)*
- The Turtle (#22)
- Knee Lift (#23)
- Half Knee Thrust (#24)
- Full Knee Thrust (#25)*
- Lateral Control (#31)*

These 30-second Quickies are listed according to their order in the full surfing workout section. They are not ordered by level of difficulty (the easiest are probably #8, Footwork and #22, The Turtle). Some of them are best done after a brief warmup; these are indicated by an asterisk *.

The suggested warmup (Four-point Stretch, #3) is a good one to use on the beach right before paddling out.

Four-point Stretch (#3): use as a quick warmup as needed. For details, see full surfing workout section.

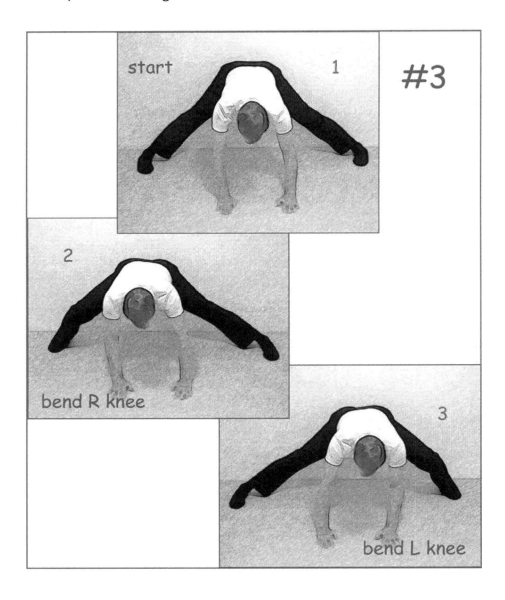

Footwork (#8): generally requires no warmup. For details, see full surfing workout section.

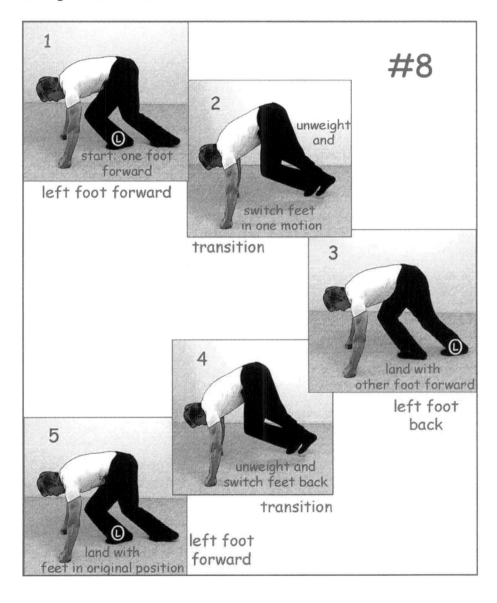

Cross-over (#9) : generally requires no warmup. For details, see full surfing workout section.

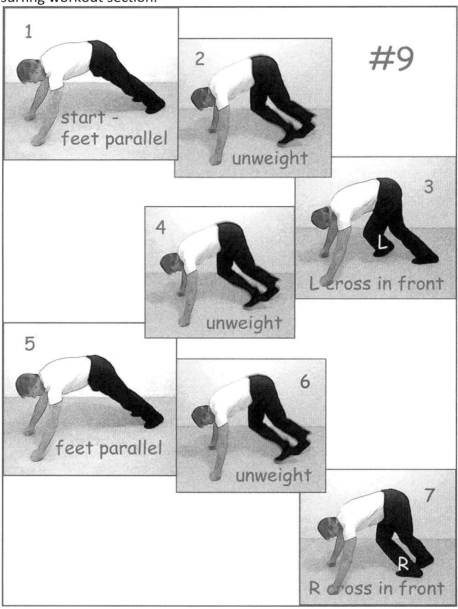

Pop-up from Knees (#11) : Suggested warmup: Four-point Stretch (#3). For details, see full surfing workout section.

Cross-step (#12): Suggested warmup: Four-point Stretch (#3). For details, see full surfing workout section.

Pop-up to Knees (#15) : Suggested warmup: Four-point Stretch (#3). For details, see full surfing workout section.

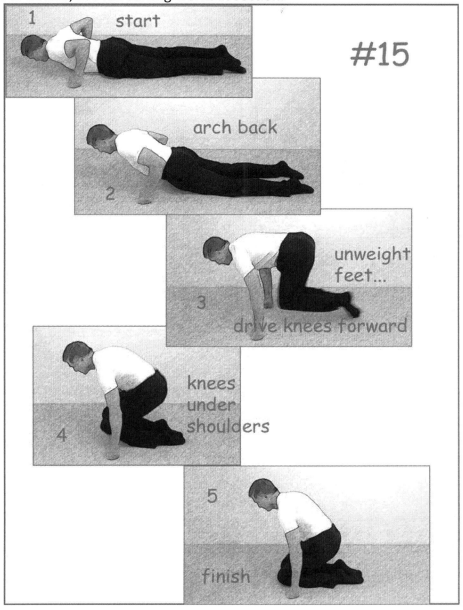

Full Pop-up (#16) : Suggested warmup: Four-point Stretch (#3). For details, see full surfing workout section.

Twisting Pop-up (#17) : Suggested warmup: Four-point Stretch (#3). For details, see full surfing workout section.

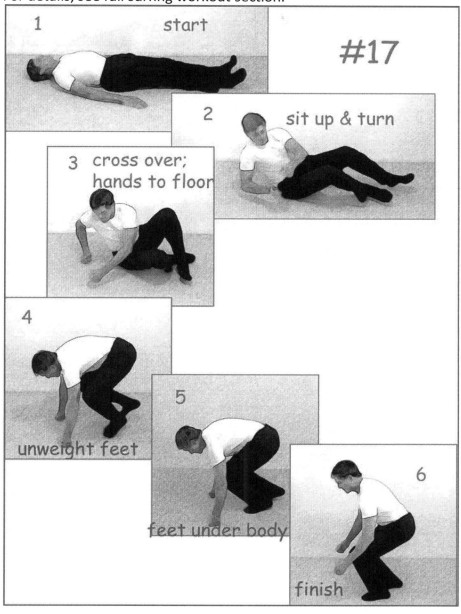

Turtle (#22) : generally requires no warmup.   For details, see full surfing workout section.

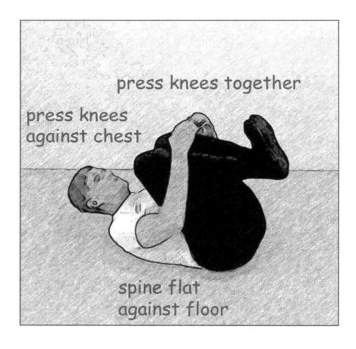

Knee Lift (#23) : generally requires no warmup. For details, see full
surfing workout section.

Half Knee Thrust (#24) : generally requires no warmup. For details, see full surfing workout section.

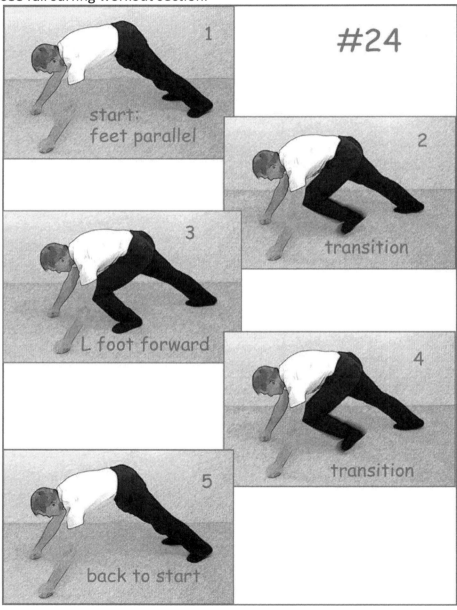

Knee Thrust (#25): Suggested warmup: Four-point Stretch (#3). For details, see full surfing workout section.

Lateral Control (#31) : Suggested warmup: Four-point Stretch (#3). For details, see full surfing workout section.

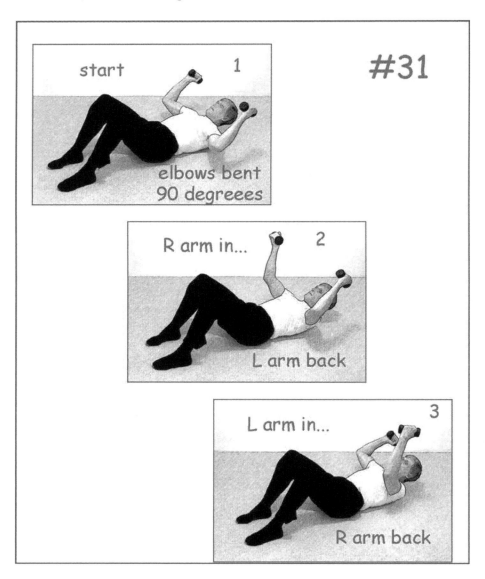

Basic 15-Minute Surfing Training Package

You can mix and match the 36-plus different exercises in this book in any way that works for you, in order to create training packages for specific purposes and objectives, and to meet your individual needs and goals. And you can alter them at any time to suit the circumstances—maybe you're coming off an injury or illness, or maybe you're traveling and don't have access to any weights. Or perhaps you're using water-filled dumbbells that are a bit lighter than your usual 3-pound weights, so you're doing more repetitions to compensate.

To show you what type of package you might create, the following pages contain a complete surfing workout that takes about 15 minutes and will give you all the strength, conditioning and flexibility needed to surf better, stronger, smarter and longer. You can do this on a daily basis, regardless of whether or not you surf that day. If you do surf that day, this gets you warmed up and limber before you leave the house; if you don't surf that day you're maintaining a very adequate level of fitness for your next session.

The 15-minute package is laid out on the next four pages. It's best to start with the first exercise (a) on the first page, and follow the alphabetical sequence. This sequence allows you to start off easily and get warmed up adequately before moving on to more demanding exercises. You start by working and stretching the legs, lower torso and body core. Then you progress to the upper body, shoulders and arms. You finish with full-body action. Notice that Shoulder Stretch (#6) is repeated, before and after the exercises with weights.

The illustrations in the 15-minute training section are merely to remind you which exercise to do. For details, see the full exercise illustrations and discussions in the main Surfing Workout section above. To make it easy for you to do this, the exercise numbers have been included below for reference.

a (#20)

15-minute workout: start with letter a

b (#21)

letters (a,b,c...) indicate sequence to follow

c (#22)

numbers (#20,#21...) indicate number in main workout section

d (#19)

e (#1)

15-minute workout (continued)

letters (f,g,h,i...) indicate sequence to follow

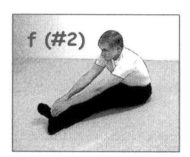

f (#2)

g (#17)

h (#3)

numbers (#2,#17...) indicate number in main workout section

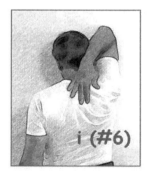

i (#6)

letters
(j,k,l,m...)
indicate
sequence
to follow

(#26)

15-minute
workout
(continued)

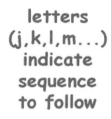

k

(#32)

l

(#36)

numbers
(#26,#32...)
indicate
number
in main
workout
section

m

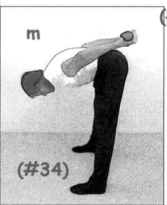

(#34)

n

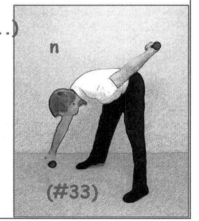

(#33)

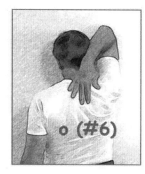

o (#6)

letters (o,p,q) indicate sequence to follow

15-minute workout (continued)

numbers (#6,#23,#12) indicate number in main workout section

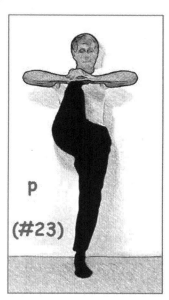

p

(#23)

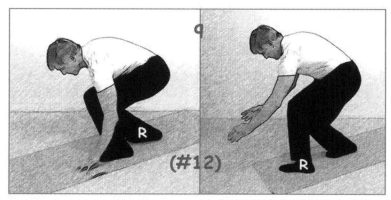

q

R

(#12)

R

PUTTING IT ALL TOGETHER

Remember your hypothetical not-so-good session at a new break? You learned a lesson from that. This time you've not only gotten in shape, you've done all your homework, and some on-site research as well.

You checked the break at maximum low tide, making mental notes of the reefs and shallows, as well as channels. You looked again at higher tide when there was a lot of swell, paying attention to reef boils, rips, and other indications of contours affecting the waves. You determined which rips could give you a free ride out through the surf zone—without dragging you over a shallow reef.

You made mental notes of which boils could be used as catapults, and which ones marked the end of the runway. You also noted boils that could serve to indicate secondary breaks where you might set up under different conditions—or could mark submerged reefs that you might have to take into account when riding a wave.

In addition, you considered tide levels and swell direction each time you looked at the break, so that you would have an idea of the best tides and swells for surfing it. You paid attention to buoy readings, and got an idea of what different breaks look like on different swell and wind directions, both individually and compared to each other.

You've also decided to be prepared for the unexpected, so that you won't be getting your leash caught on a rock (or wrapped around your feet), whether in or out of the water. You may have decided to leave the leash off when surfing a break with a lot of kelp and seaweed in the water, since you can get hooked up on it while paddling, taking off or riding a wave.

You've also done some other thinking on your own. You may check surf forecasts, but you'll pay more attention to your own wave knowledge, observation, and common sense. You'll keep improving by practicing at least one technical point during every session—and you'll have the good sense to recognize your own limits and avoid putting others at risk by surfing beyond your current skill level around other surfers.

And you haven't ignored the human element. You're going to make sure that you don't incur needless hostility by being a wave hog or drop-in artist, or letting go of your board right in front of another surfer. You're not going to show up with a posse, or create one by calling all your buddies by cellphone. You've realized that if you're competent, sensible, and mindful of surfing etiquette, you've earned the right to be in the lineup at any break you choose to surf.

You're good to go.

THE PAYOFF

Apart from the workouts—which could be used for any sport, or for no sport, simply to keep you healthy, flexible and strong—why should this book exist at all? Why pay attention to surfing? In other words, why surf?

A writer who fulfilled a lifelong dream by taking art lessons described this issue very well. He had been fascinated with the concept of being able to use a pencil and a sheet of paper to create reality: an image, either of something real or something imagined that looked real. But he found—as people find with all sorts of activities, from art to music to cooking—that once he mastered the skill, the magic disappeared. It's an old, old story: what you don't have or can't do seems wonderful beyond belief, but when you have it or can do it, somehow the thrill is gone. And then it's on to the Next Great Thing.

Surfing is qualitatively different.

Partly, perhaps, because surfing is multidimensional. Surfing is, first and foremost, the art of blending harmoniously with nature in the form of a fast-moving wave. At the same time, it's also a contest, a test of your ability both to anticipate and to react correctly to an opponent a million times quicker, more powerful and more unpredictable than any living adversary could ever be.

In a way, it's like hunting: finding a likely spot for waves, picking the best place to lie in wait, scanning the horizon for a set, making final adjustments, and catching the wave you've selected. Even the terminology of "catching" or "getting" a wave implies a sort of craftiness. And, as in big-game hunting, sometimes you get the wave, and sometimes the wave gets you. To quote one young and talented surfer on why he loves it so, "You have to be smarter than the wave."

Finally, surfing is—permit me a high-flown metaphor—a window on eternity. From the moment you pick a wave and begin to paddle for it, time stops. You are caught up in a swirl of pure energy and experience that excludes everything else. You have no age, no identity, no desire other than to stay in the endless moment of the now.

It doesn't get any better than that.

ABOUT THE AUTHOR

Dave Rearwin grew up surfing in Southern California in the 1950s with a crew that included legends like Rick Naish, Carl Ekstrom and Butch Van Artsdalen. He transitioned from balsa to foam, from longboards to shortboards, and from the no-leash, no-wetsuit era to the ease and comfort we enjoy today.

Sidelined by sports injuries, he developed a series of non-destructive, zero-impact, surf-specific exercises (many derived from physical therapy workouts) that allowed him to get back into surfing after a layoff of several years. These are the exercises that form the core of this book.

Made in the USA
San Bernardino, CA
01 November 2012